ASEAN-Korea Relations

Security, Trade and Community Building

EDITED BY **Ho Khai Leong**

ISEAS

Institute of Southeast Asian Studies
Singapore

First published in Singapore in 2007 by ISEAS Publishing
Institute of Southeast Asian Studies
30 Heng Mui Keng Terrace
Pasir Panjang
Singapore 119614

E-mail: publish@iseas.edu.sg
Website: http://bookshop.iseas.edu.sg

The responsibility for facts and opinions is this publication rests exclusively with the authors and their interpretations do not necessarily reflect the views or the policy of the publisher or its supporters.

ISEAS Library Cataloguing-in-Publication Data

ASEAN–Korea relations : security, trade, and community building / edited by Ho Khai Leong.
   1.   National security—Southeast Asia.
   2.   National security—Korea.
   3.   Southeast Asia—Foreign economic relations—Korea.
   4.   Korea—Foreign economic relations—Southeast Asia.
   5.   Southeast Asia—Foreign relations—Korea.
   6.   Korea—Foreign relations—Southeast Asia.
   I.   Ho, Khai Leong, 1954-
UA833.5   A841   2007

ISBN-13:   978-981-230-406-3   (hard cover—13 digit)
ISBN-10:   981-230-406-1   (hard cover—10 digit)
ISBN-13:   978-981-230-655-5   (PDF—13 digit)
ISBN-10:   981-230-655-2   (PDF—10 digit)

Typeset by Gantec Publishing
Printed in Singapore by Photoplates Pte Ltd

Contents

trade with Singapore, as the latter has become a springboard for South Korean businesses to launch their produce into the emerging ASEAN market. With the conclusion of the FTA, economic co-operation will be expanded and strengthened.

Our two countries have many things in common: an information/ knowledge-based market economy, excellent human resources, a democracy and liberty, and the aspiration of becoming a regional hub. Korea is pursuing a "Policy of Peace and Prosperity" as it seeks to become a Northeast Asia regional hub. In that process, we are eager to share knowledge with Singapore, which is already a leading regional hub.

As an engine of growth and development, a technological economic hub in Northeast Asia and Southeast Asia will contribute to Asia's future prosperity.

Korea and Singapore have worked together to improve co-operation among East Asian countries in summits such as ASEAN plus Three, ASEAN Regional Forum (ARF), Asia-Pacific Economic Co-operation (APEC), and Asia–Europe Meeting (ASEM). We hope that such efforts for establishing an East Asian community will be fulfilled in the near future, as it will benefit Korea, Singapore, and our neighbouring countries. In this century of globalization, a country's size is immaterial, as this is the age of innovation, creative thinking, and the power of the mind. In this respect, our two countries can play a very unique role in shaping an "Asian era".

In addition, we can explore other areas of co-operation in the area of human security. Jointly Korea and Singapore should co-operate in dealing with piracy, the safety of the sea lines of communication, organized crime, illegal migration, human trafficking, and above all, terrorism. These are very serious threats to both our countries and people. Co-operation between our two countries will make the world a safer and more peaceful place.

There is an old Korean saying that goes, "A good friend makes your journey short and comfortable". I hope the conference, and the resultant book, will contribute significantly to our prosperous future.

Han Tae-kyu
Chancellor
Institute of Foreign Affairs and
National Security, Korea

Foreword

Korea has been a dialogue partner of ASEAN since July 1991, and through the ASEAN plus Three multilateral framework of East Asian co-operation, it now meets regularly with ASEAN at summit levels. ASEAN members regard it as a valuable contributing partner. In November 1989 Korea and ASEAN established a Sectoral Dialogue relationship. In July 1991 the relationship was moved up to Full Dialogue Partnership. In these dialogues mutual support for moving towards strengthened Korea–ASEAN co-operation was reaffirmed.

However, the level of public awareness of Korea in ASEAN remains low. Asian attention on the Korean Peninsula has been fairly parochial, with much focus on the vicissitudes in its security environment — weapons of mass destruction (WMD), nuclear proliferation, and problems in the north. In the light of this the image of Korea is inevitably skewed or distorted. Despite the popularity of Korean movies and actors and actresses — a new cultural phenomenon sweeping Asia, aptly called "The Korean Wave" (in Korean, *Hallyu*) — among citizens in ASEAN countries in recent years, our understanding of Korea needs to be further enhanced.

The security environment in East Asia features prominently in our discussions of geopolitics. Within the East Asian equation, the Korea factor was overshadowed by Japan at one time, and now ever increasingly, by a rising China. The ASEAN public image of Korea was equally skewed in the post-11 September era as well as the years following the onslaught of the Asian financial/economic crisis. The after-effects of these incidents of economic and political turbulence have not dissipated, and ASEAN has far from recovered its pre-Asian financial crisis economic turnovers.

These images belie the realities of growing interdependence between ASEAN and Korea, for the latter is a member of the ASEAN Regional Forum (ARF), an ASEAN dialogue partner, and a player in the ASEAN plus Three. Furthermore, the ASEAN states and Korea are members of the Asia-Pacific Economic Co-operation (APEC). Korea and ASEAN have jointly executed over 100 co-operation projects since 1990 in the areas of trade, investment, tourism, technology transfer, and the fostering of human resources. Globalization has brought Northeast and Southeast Asia much closer together, leading to expectations of an emerging East Asian integration process, and kindling hopes for an East Asian community.

In October 1994, the Institute of Southeast Asian Studies (ISEAS) organized the first Korea–ASEAN conference in Singapore to look into the emerging issues in trade and investment relations between Korea and ASEAN. The conference proceedings were published in the ISEAS publication, *ASEAN and Korea: Emerging Issues in Trade and Investment Relations* the following year. That first Korea–ASEAN conference was followed by another conference in Seoul in co-operation with the Korean Association of Southeast Asian Studies. The book compiling the papers presented at the second Korea–ASEAN conference, *ASEAN and Korea: Trends in Economic and Labour Relations,* was published by ISEAS in 1997.

In the ensuing years both the ASEAN region and Korea have experienced momentous developments — 11 September, the wars in Afghanistan and Iraq, the rising spectre of new transnational threats, foremost of which is international terrorism, the reorientation of America's international security role and attendant impacts on friends and allies, and regional expansion on the ASEAN side. These events have resulted in changes in North and South Korean relations, stagnation in the Japanese economy, the rising economic profile of China, and changing patterns of international economic relations.

These developments have had various impacts on Korea and ASEAN countries; and as such, call for a much-needed re-examination of the political and economic realities governing the ASEAN–Korea relationship.

In recent times ISEAS has successfully organized international forums and conferences on ASEAN–Japan, ASEAN–India, and ASEAN–China relations. Singapore has also successfully negotiated a bilateral free trade agreement (FTA) with Korea, and is in fact tasked to lead the ASEAN side in the upcoming ASEAN–Korea FTA talks.

ISEAS has had the great honour of fostering this spirit of co-operation when it jointly organized with Korea's Institute of Foreign Affairs and National Security (IFANS), the Conference on Strengthening the Korea–ASEAN Relationship on 15 September 2005 in Singapore, with generous funding from the Korea Foundation. This book is the product of the conference. Even as we try to cope with unfolding events, some of the analysis published now may have been dated by events that happened over the last one year. We are most fortunate to have had the opportunity to co-operate with our Korean counterparts in promoting Korea–ASEAN dialogue, and hope to continue this effort in the future.

K. Kesavapany
Director
Institute of Southeast Asian Studies

Acknowledgements

In 2004 the Institute of Southeast Asian Studies (ISEAS), Singapore, launched a series of seminars and conferences on the relations between ASEAN and the regional powers. So far, the conferences on ASEAN–China, ASEAN–India, ASEAN–Australia and New Zealand, and ASEAN–Russia have been held. The proceedings of these conferences were subsequently published by ISEAS Publishing. The present volume on ASEAN–Korea relations is a continuous effort in the research programme. The papers in this volume were first presented at the Conference on Strengthening the Korea–ASEAN Relationship, held on 15 September 2005 in Singapore. The conference was jointly organized by ISEAS, Singapore, and the Institute of Foreign Affairs and National Security (IFANS), Seoul, Korea, with generous funding from the Korea Foundation.

The theme chosen for the conference was "Strengthening the Korea–ASEAN Relationship", with sub-themes focusing on regional security, economic co-operation, and community building. ISEAS played the role of co-ordinating and inviting scholars from ASEAN to write on the respective themes, and IFANS co-ordinated the logistics of inviting the Korean counterparts to Singapore.

The editor owes a tremendous debt of gratitude to all of the distinguished authors for their patience and willingness to update their work. I owe an equal debt to Ambassador Han Tae-kyu, Chancellor, IFANS, Korea; Ambassador Kim Seung-eui, Executive Vice President, Korea Foundation; Ryu Kwang-sok, South Korea's Ambassador to Singapore; and Jeong Woo-jin, First Secretary, Korean Embassy in Singapore. They were instrumental in making the conference possible and assisted in every responsible way to co-ordinate with ISEAS staff. I am also deeply appreciative of K. Kesavapany, Director, and Chin Kin Wah, Deputy Director, ISEAS, for their initiative and support throughout the project. Thanks also go to Chang Chiou Yi and Ng Boon

Yian, research associates at ISEAS and rapporteurs of the conference, for their excellent executive summary; Toh Mun Heng and Rodolfo Severino for lending valuable assistance during the conference; ISEAS secretary staff, particularly Betty Kwan, for their capable administrative finesse; Sharon Loo for going through some of the chapters; Triena Ong, Managing Editor at ISEAS, for her assistance and patience while I went through drafts and solved the typical problems associated with putting together a collection of conference papers.

Ho Khai Leong

The Contributors

BAE Geung-Chan is Professor, Institute of Foreign Affairs and National Security (IFANS), Korea. He received his Ph.D. in Government from the Claremont Graduate School in 1988. His major research interests are ASEAN and Southeast Asian Affairs, and Regional Co-operation in East Asia. His published works in recent years include "Key Task for East Asian Regional Cooperation", "Challenges and Tasks Facing ROK-China-Japan Tripartite Cooperation: View from Recent Historical Controversies and National-ism", "Northeast Asian Cooperation Initiative and Korea's Diplomatic Tasks: A Strategy for Regional Cooperation", and "Prospects for the East Asian Summit".

Kang CHOI is Professor, Institute of Foreign Affairs and National Security (IFANS), Korea. He earned his Ph.D. in Political Science from the Ohio State University in 1991, M.A. from the University of Wisconsin-Madison in 1985, and B.A. from Kyunghee University in 1983. His published works include "An Approach toward a Common Form of Defense White Paper", "International Arms Control and Inter-Korean Arms Control", "Inter-Korean Arms Control and Implications for the USFK", "Future ROK-US Security Alliance", "A New Approach toward Inter-Korean Arms Control", and "North Korea's Intentions and Strategies on Nuclear Game".

HAN Tae-kyu is the Chancellor, Institute of Foreign Affairs and National Security (IFANS), Korea. He previously served as Ambassador to Greece and Bangladesh.

HERNANDEZ, Carolina G. is Professor of Political Science at the University of the Philippines. She holds the degrees of Bachelor of Science in Foreign

Service (*cum laude*) from the University of the Philippines, Masters in International Relations (First in First Class) from the University of Karachi, and Ph.D. in Political Science from the State University of New York at Buffalo. Her latest edited volumes are (with Gill Wilkins) *Population, Food, Energy and the Environment* (a CAEC publication for the 2000 Seoul ASEM Summit), and a trilogy (on Environment, People, and Globalization) with David Dewitt entitled *Development and Security in Southeast Asia* (Ashgate, 2003).

KAMARULNIZAM Abdullah is Associate Professor at the Strategic and International Relations Programme, School of History, Politics, and Strategic Studies at the Faculty of Social Sciences and Humanities, University Kebangsaan Malaysia. He obtained his Ph.D. in Politics from Lancaster University, United Kingdom. His main research interests are political violence, religious militancy, and national security issues that are pertinent to Malaysia and the Southeast Asian region. His latest publication is "Islamic Militancy in Malaysia" in *The Making of Ethnic and Religious Conflict in Southeast Asia: Cases and Resolutions*, edited by Lambang Trijuno. Yogyakarta: Centre for Security and Peace Studies, Gadjah Mada University, 2004.

K. KESAVAPANY is Director of the Institute of Southeast Asian Studies, Singapore. Prior to this, he was Singapore's High Commissioner to Malaysia from 1997 to 2002. He also served as Singapore's Permanent Representative to the United Nations in Geneva and concurrently accredited as Ambassador to Italy and Turkey. He was elected as the first Chairman of the General Council of the World Trade Organization (WTO) when it was established in January 1995. He graduated from the University of Malaya with a Bachelor of Arts (Honours) degree and obtained a Master of Arts degree from the School of Oriental and African Studies, University of London.

Yul KWON is a research fellow at the Korea Institute for International Economic Policy (KIEP) in Seoul, Korea. He is currently Head of Research Division in charge of Southeast and South Asian Studies. He received his Ph.D. in economics from Sogang University in Seoul, focusing on development economics and international economics. He has published several journal articles and books, including *A Study on the Poverty Reduction Strategy of Southeast Asian Countries* (2004), *East Asian Regionalism Focusing on ASEAN Plus Three* (2004), and *ASEAN's Economic Integration: Recent Development and Policy Implications* (2003). His research interests include Southeast Asian economies, Asian transitional economies, and Korea's ODA policy.

Seo-Hang LEE is the Dean of Research, Institute of Foreign Affairs and National Security (IFANS), Korea. He received his Ph.D. from Kent State University and B.A. and M.A. from Seoul National University. He is Co-Chairman of the Council for Security Co-operation in the Asia-Pacific, Korea. In 1995 and 2000, respectively, he was a member of the Korean delegation at the Fifth and Sixth NPT conference in New York. He has published or edited more than seventy monographs and books on international security issues and ocean politics. His recent articles include "The North Korean Question in the Northeast Asian Security Arrangement" (2004) and "Maritime Strategy of the Republic of Korea" (2002).

Chanin MEPHOKEE is Associate Professor, Faculty of Economics at Thammasat University, Thailand. He received his B.A. in Economics from Thammasat University, Thailand, M.A. in Economics from the University of Michigan, United States, and Ph.D. in Economics from the University of Kansas, United States. He was a member of the Thailand–U.S. FTA Negotiation Task Force, Ministry of Foreign Affairs.

Innwon PARK is Professor of International Economics in the Division of International Studies at Korea University. He received his B.A. and M.A. in Economics from Korea University and his Ph.D. in Economics from the University of Pennsylvania in 1993. From 1993 to 1998, he worked as an assistant professor in the Department of Economics at the National University of Singapore. He is specialized in the quantitative analysis of economic integration among countries in East Asia and the CGE (Computable General Equilibrium) modelling.

Sung-Hoon PARK is Professor of Economics and International Trade at the Graduate School of International Studies (GSIS), Korea University. He has held research fellowship at the Korea Institute for International Economic Policy (KIEP), and visiting professorships at Macau Institute of European Studies, Ritsumeikan University, and ASEF University. For the 2003/04 academic year, he was awarded a Fulbright Visiting Scholarship to the Graduate School of International Relations and Pacific Studies (IR/PS) at the University of California, San Diego, United States. He has been doing research on international trade policy, European and Asian economic integration, and Korea's external economic policies.

Edy PRASETYONO is the Head of Department of International Relations, CSIS, Indonesia. He obtained his Ph.D. from the Department of Political

Science and International Studies, Birmingham University, England, in 2001. He is a member of the Indonesian Committee, Council for Security Co-operation in the Asia-Pacific. He has been active in several projects on security sector reform in Indonesia, including memberships in working groups drafting armed forces bill, defence white paper, and Strategic Defence Review of the Department of Defence. His areas of interest include ASEAN, security issues in the Asia-Pacific, defence and military studies, and European affairs.

Le Dinh TINH is Deputy Director of the Department of International Co-operation and Administration, Vietnam. He received his M.P.A. from the University of Hawaii at Manoa and B.A. in International Politics from the Hanoi Institute for International Relations (IIR). Prior to his current job, he was a research fellow at the IIR. His most recent publication is "US-Southeast Asia Security Relationship Revisited", *International Studies*, IIR.

The Editor

HO Khai Leong is Associate Professor at the School of Humanities and Social Sciences, Nanyang Technological University, Singapore, and visiting fellow at the Institute of Southeast Asian Studies, Singapore. He obtained his Ph.D. in Political Science from the Ohio State University, United States. His current research interests include Malaysia and Singapore politics, China–ASEAN relations, corporate governance, and administrative reforms. His latest publications include *China and Southeast Asia: Global Changes and Regional Challenges* (co-editor and contributor), *Reforming Corporate Governance in Southeast Asia: Economics, Politics and Regulations* (editor and contributor), and *Rethinking Administrative Reforms in Southeast Asia* (editor and contributor).

1
Introduction

Ho Khai Leong

ASEAN–KOREA RELATIONS: PARTNERSHIP IN COMMUNITY BUILDING

The relations between the Association of Southeast Asian Nations (ASEAN) and the Republic of Korea (ROK) occupy a somewhat awkward position in the Asia-Pacific foreign relations *vis-à-vis* ASEAN–Japan and ASEAN–China relations. For the past decades, the focus of the Southeast Asian region has been on Japan, as the latter has been taking the leadership role in the region's economic development through investment and foreign aid. Japanese cultural influences have also been prevalent in almost every corner of Southeast Asia, and the recent surge of Japanese military nationalism, once again, has become a concern for the Southeast Asian governments and citizens. The rise of China in the 1990s quickly propelled Southeast Asian governments and policy-makers to re-examine its potential political, economic, and strategic impacts. Intellectual as well as institutional attention on a rising China and Sino–ASEAN relations has since blossomed into a flourishing enterprise.

In the midst of these regional dynamics, ASEAN–Korea relations seem relatively neglected, and have been relegated to receiving marginal policy attention from Southeast Asian governments. As the ROK is a latecomer in establishing ties with its Southeast Asian neighbours, it needs to catch up with the other two Northeast Asian neighbours in building and improving ASEAN relations. The free trade agreement (FTA) between China and ASEAN has been in effect since July 2004. After signing bilateral trade agreements with

Singapore, Thailand, Malaysia, and the Philippines, Japan is seeking an accord with ASEAN. With most of its Asian neighbours already on the FTA bandwagon, the ROK is further pressed to speedily complete its bilateral accord with ASEAN. At present, the ROK has only signed an FTA with one ASEAN country, Singapore.

ASEAN–Korea relations have improved markedly since the 1960s and continue to grow stronger. Given this era of regionalism and globalization, it would not be farfetched to speculate that ASEAN and Korea could share similar fates. Furthermore, if ASEAN were to seriously confront the opportunities and challenges at both the global and regional levels, it would have to bring in all the major powers in the region. ASEAN is able to do so through the Ten plus One (ASEAN plus China) and the Ten plus Three (ASEAN plus China, Japan, and Korea) frameworks. Indeed, it is difficult to envision a progressive and stable East Asia without a significant involvement of the ROK in the long run. Its political and economic relations with its Northeast Asian neighbours render it the ideal anchor for a stable Asia.

ASEAN has come to factor greatly in Korea's strategic and economic consideration as its policy-makers reflect on its regional and global positions. On 15 December 2005 Korea took a major step forward in its pursuit of FTAs by signing the framework agreement with ASEAN — the ASEAN–South Korea FTA (AKFTA). Although meaningful negotiations would only be completed by the end of 2006, the agreement provided new momentum for further Korean talks with more trading partners such as the United States, Japan, and China. With this preliminary FTA negotiation with ASEAN, the ROK is expected to compete with China and Japan on a level playing field.

The AKFTA has far-reaching significance for the ROK, as its matured economy is now provided with many opportunities to contribute to the formation of an Asian community. The general push towards greater economic integration came in the wake of the failed World Trade Organization (WTO) ministerial meeting in Cancun, Mexico, in September 2003, when a number of countries were looking to strengthen their trading positions through bilateral and regional deals. The East Asia Community idea — based on the three pillars of economic co-operation, political and security co-operation, and socio-cultural co-operation — sought to converge all the major Asian powers' interests so as to negotiate for a deal benefiting all. The ultimate goal of the community is to create a competitive region with a free flow of investment, goods, services, and skilled labour combined with a freer flow of capital, stable and equitable economic development, and reduced poverty and socio-economic disparities by 2020. These goals are challenges for ASEAN and the ROK, requiring the joint commitment of their peoples and governments.

ORGANIZATION OF THE BOOK

Both ASEAN and Korea rate regional and domestic security a top concern. Despite the different sets of security challenges confronting Southeast Asia and Northeast Asia, they face certain commonalities. Kamarulnizam's chapter entitled "Southeast Asian Security Challenges: A Strategic View from ASEAN" details the security challenges ASEAN currently faces and the resolution of potential conflict areas if the region is to move forward. The manner in which Southeast Asia handles itself in the aftermath of the 11 September attacks hinges on its ability to amicably manage some of the contentious issues threatening regional stability and peace. Seo-Hang Lee's chapter, "Changing Security Environments in Northeast Asia: A Korean View", describes the complex security environments in Northeast Asia, and argues that they have at least three features: first, the deep suspicions among the states; second, the anxiety of the regimes for political survival; and third, the existence of alliance and alignment. While observers do look on the recent developments in the region optimistically, increased intra-regional economic interdependence has to be acknowledged.

Both ASEAN and Korea face pressing problems relating to non-traditional security issues. These include terrorism, drug-trafficking, maritime piracy, and infectious diseases. These non-traditional security problems transcend national and regional borders, making them too difficult for one country to tackle alone. Carolina Hernandez argues in "Strengthening ASEAN–Korea Co-operation in Non-Traditional Security Issues" that there are indeed differences between ASEAN and Korean perspectives on non-traditional security issues. However, these differences should not impede co-operation in combating these problems. Kang Choi, on the other hand, chooses to focus on terrorism as a global issue. He distinguishes "new terrorism" from traditional terrorism, by stating that the former takes advantage of the increased vulnerability of states due to growing interdependence and interconnectedness. It also strikes indiscriminately, creating casualties and inflicting horrifying damages. Although the author suggests various ways of international co-operation to counter terrorism, he cautions that "imposing our own values and ideas upon the others" should be avoided.

In the light of the rush to complete FTAs in the region, it is unsurprising to find that trade and economic co-operation is another major theme in ASEAN–Korea relations. Chanin Mephokee's chapter, "ASEAN–Korea Economic Co-operation: Thailand's Perspectives", provides an overview of the Korean rationales for signing FTAs with ASEAN. Trade volume and value between ASEAN and Korea has been growing remarkably. The next logical step in this relationship would be to establish the AKFTA so that both parties would have more open access to each other's markets. The Korean scholars concur with this assessment. Yul Kwon and Innwon Park argue that the focus in the future should be deeper integration of the two sides, taking into account the different and sometimes sensitive economic levels and sectors. Once this is achieved, the AKFTA could eventually expand into an FTA encompassing East Asia in its entirety.

While the organized front of ASEAN gives the appearance of a coherent whole, there remain many differences in the region's level of economic and social development. Consequently, discussions on community building and economic co-operation ought to take such differences into consideration. Priorities and due considerations should be given to Cambodia, Laos, Myanmar, and Vietnam (CLMV). It is in this spirit that special attention is given to these countries in the discussion on community building in East Asia. Le Dinh Tinh's chapter, "ASEAN–Korea Co-operation in the Development of New ASEAN Members", argues that Korea could offer CLMV assistance in institutional building and human resource development, thereby narrowing the biggest obstacle to further regional integration — the development gap. Sung-Hoon Park's chapter focuses on Korea's Official Development Assistance (ODA) policy towards CLMV. While the overall strategic direction of Korea's developmental assistance programmes to developing countries is generally positive, Park suggests that there are still a few challenges for Korea's ODA policy in the following matters — its decision to join the Development Assistance Committee (DAC) of the Organization for Economic Co-operation and Development (OECD), upgrading of ODA policy, and intensifying its efforts to help CLMV in ASEAN.

Greater strategic and economic co-operation undoubtedly culminates in deeper integration and community building. Edy Prasetyono's chapter explores the range of security co-operation options available to both Korea and ASEAN in their mutual desire to strengthen East Asia integration. He argues that political commitment is necessary, and ASEAN and Korea should learn from the Asia-Pacific Economic Co-operation (APEC) experience, which many felt was a disappointing mechanism for integration. Bae Geung-Chan, however, is much more optimistic. In the chapter entitled "ASEAN and Korea in East Asian Co-operation", Bae points out that while there are great power rivalries in the region, regional co-operative mechanisms, such as ASEAN plus Three and the East Asia Summit, could be an effective way of reducing tensions and preventing potential conflicts among countries in the region.

ASEAN–KOREA RELATIONS: WHERE DO WE GO FROM HERE?

It is quite clear that as ASEAN's ties with key regional partners deepen, Korea will emerge as a pillar for economic integration in Asia, linking China, India, and Southeast Asia. As the AKFTA is expected to commence in 2006 under the timetable proposed by the ASEAN–Korea Experts Group (AKEG), the FTA negotiations may be completed in two years or by 2007. The AKFTA is expected to be realized by 2009, a year earlier than the ASEAN–China FTA (which is expected to be implemented in 2010).

As both sides prepare for a future of a freer trade through multilateral mechanisms or bilateral trade agreements, the governments involved will have to strengthen the competitiveness of their domestic industries. Some of the ASEAN states will have to pay special attention to their agriculture and service sectors. Korean bilateral relations with individual ASEAN states will also be watched closely by those states with unique developmental needs and interests. For example, Thailand is still perturbed by its ongoing dispute with Korea over rice import, as the latter has sought to keep out Thai rice imports through high tariffs.

It is hoped that meetings between ASEAN and Korea's economic ministers will be regularized. After fifteen years of formal ASEAN–Korea relations, this will be a major step forward. While non-official ties between the two sides have continued to grow, increased governmental contacts will certainly add more substance to the already blossoming relationship. There is no doubt that the influx of businesses from Korea to ASEAN, and *vice versa*, would hugely enhance the competitiveness, the innovation capability, and profitability of the whole East Asia. Indeed, the two sides can join forces *to act*, and in time to come, they would undoubtedly become the indispensable vehicle of East Asian economic growth.

REFERENCES

Ho Khai Leong and Samuel Ku, eds. *China and Southeast Asia. Global Changes and Regional Challenges*. Singapore: Institute of Southeast Asian Studies, 2005.

Saw Swee-Hock, Sheng Lijun, and Chin Kin Wah, eds. *ASEAN–China Relations. Realities and Prospects*. Singapore: Institute of Southeast Asian Studies, 2005.

Siddique, Sharon and Sree Kumar, compilers. *The 2nd ASEAN Reader*. Singapore: Institute of Southeast Asian Studies, 2003.

PART I

Overview of Respective Regional Security Environments and Security Challenges

2
Southeast Asian Security Challenges: A Strategic View from ASEAN

Kamarulnizam Abdullah

INTRODUCTION

Since the end of the Cold War more than a decade ago, several dynamic new security measures have been introduced in Southeast Asia. The direction of these security measures neither alters the region's geo-political position and relations within the region, nor the region's relations with the external powers.[1] It can be argued that despite the political problems faced by Indonesia and other Cold War's leftover regional conflicts such as the Aceh and Mindanao issues, Southeast Asia is relatively stable. Although the region faces the growing threats of Muslim terrorism, there have been so far no major inter-state conflicts. On the whole, outstanding bilateral issues have been negotiated and resolved amicably. Malaysia and Indonesia, for instance, managed to resolve their overlapping claims over Sipadan and Ligitan islands through the International Court of Justice (ICJ). Although the loss of Sipadan and Ligitan created political pressures on the Indonesian Government to protect the country's sovereignty and interest, relations between Indonesia and Malaysia are unaffected. Similarly, while other bilateral overlapping claims such as over Pedra Branca (Malaysia–Singapore) and Ambalat (Malaysia–Indonesia) arguably have created political tension, they have not aversely affected the relations between the conflicting parties. The reason for this political maturity among Asian states is their growing regional integration through ASEAN. ASEAN has ensured that the negotiating process continues.

Generally speaking, Southeast Asian countries, unlike those in East Asia, tend to have more co-operative inter-state relations because they share a common history of colonialism. The countries in Southeast Asia, except Thailand, were colonized by the European imperialist powers of Britain, the Netherlands, Portugal, and France. Furthermore, unlike states in East Asia, the Southeast Asian countries, with the exception of Cambodia, were never invaded by their neighbours; nor did they have any serious conflict with each other.[2] As most of the Southeast Asian countries had faced communist-led domestic insurgencies, their security concerns tend to revolve around domestic consolidation, stability, and regime survival.[3] The process of consultation, negotiation, and bargaining therefore becomes a crucial political tool in the region's inter-state relations.

East Asian countries, on the other hand, tend to have realist biases in their attitudes towards military power and development. Their approaches towards conflict management and resolution have been conditioned by their histories and experiences in war. Several parts of the People's Republic of China (PRC), for instance, were annexed by Western imperialist powers during the final days of the Qing dynasty and also by Japanese military imperialism in the nineteenth and mid-twentieth century. The experiences left a deep psychological scar among the people and the governing elites in the country. That is why the strategic culture of the East Asian states emphasizes the "utility of power and on the importance of maintaining balance".[4]

However, this does not mean that Southeast Asia is without any serious political or potential conflict. In the post-Cold War period, internally driven issues are the region's major security challenges. Questions of regime survival, ethnic identity, religious militancy, and political violence dominate the security agenda of regional countries. It can be argued that the post-Cold War period has borne witness to both emerging and old regional security issues with the potential to threaten regional stability if improperly addressed. The prolonged centre–periphery conflicts, such as those in southern Thailand, Aceh, and Mindanao, and the tension in the South China Sea over overlapping claims are part of the Cold War legacy and are far from over. In addition, the 11 September 2001 incident is arguably the defining moment of the post-Cold War regional politics and security. Some domestic security issues have transcended the boundaries of regional co-operation so much so that internally driven security issues are no longer considered domestic in nature.

The emergence of these new regional security concerns, such as radical political Islam, terrorism, and the piracy threats in the regional waters, require all the Southeast Asian countries' concerted effort and co-operation. These security issues cannot be treated as a Southeast Asian problem in the light of the growing economic, political, and security connections between East and Southeast Asia. This connection has been matched by "growing security interdependence, as is evident in the growing salience of problems such as territorial disputes in the South China Sea or the potential for regional hegemony by China and Japan, both of which transcend sub-regional dimensions".[5]

The major purpose of this chapter is to highlight and discuss some outstanding and newly emergent security challenges of Southeast Asia in the post-11 September 2001 world.

CONFLICTS OF ETHNIC IDENTITY AND LAND DISPUTE: OLD ISSUES, NEW DIMENSION

One of the major security challenges to the Southeast Asian security is the question of ethnic identity, which has in turn led to severe political violence. While the issue is not new to Southeast Asia, it has to be acknowledged that ethnic identity has entered a new dimension in the aftermath of the 11 September attacks on America. The conflict surrounding ethnic identity often arises from a minority group's desire for political recognition. During their countries' independence processes, these minority groups were forgotten and their political future was left to the unilateral decisions of the colonial powers. Hence, some of these minority groups were absorbed into mainstream ethnic groups and their traditional lands divided into several territories. This caused them much confusion over their own identities and political allegiances. Economic deprivation and discrimination added further insult, thereby prompting them to revolt against the regime in power.

Conflict and Violence in Southern Thailand

The conflict and violence in southern Thailand illustrates how the issue of ethnic identity came to be part of a political struggle against the state. Although earlier critics argued that the conflict had "the potential to escalate to a civil war"[and] possibly invited external support to intervene on the behalf of the minority group", the separatist activities appeared to have been curtailed.[6] The area was relatively stable (politically) in the 1980s and 1990s. This relatively peaceful period could be due to the initiatives taken by the Thai Government to support the Malay-Muslim cultural rights and religious freedom. This and the implementation of economic development in the area gave the local people confidence. Furthermore, close security co-operation with neighbouring Malaysia successfully curbed subversive activities near the Thai–Malaysian border.

During the 1980s and 1990s, attempts were made to develop the southern Thai region to reduce the locals' political opposition towards the central government. The inclusion of the southern provinces as part of the Indonesia–Malaysia–Thailand Growth Triangle (IMT-GT) was a political attempt to accelerate the economic development so as to prevent the area from lagging behind the other Thai provinces. In fact, the Malaysian and Thai Governments jointly developed a gas exploration project in the disputed territorial waters in the Gulf of Thailand as part of the IMT-GT development. The US$800 million Thai–Malaysia gas pipeline project was a 50–50 venture between Malaysia's Petronas and the Petroleum Authority of Thailand. The proposed project sought to supply gas from southern Thailand to Peninsular Malaysia from a 7,520-square-kilometre offshore oil exploration area called the Malaysia–Thailand Joint Development Area (JDA). However, the scheme encountered a setback when Thai environmentalists protested against the project, effectively delaying the construction of the proposed gas separation plant and transmission pipeline. The protest and its ensuing delay of the gas separation and pipeline project appeared to have diminished the growth triangle's objectives.

Questions of ethnic identity and political rights in southern Thailand regained momentum following two major bloody incidents in 2004. On 28 April 2004 more than thirty Muslim youths were killed when the military forces launched grenade attacks on the 425-year-old Krue Sae mosque in Pattani town. The Thai Government claimed that the youths were responsible for a series of attacks on ten police stations and check-points in an effort to steal weapons.[7] Critics, however, argued that the security forces had carried out a cold-blooded massacre in order to teach Islamic separatists a lesson.[8] In another incident on 25 October 2004 riots broke out in Tak Bai, a small town in Narathiwat, southern Thailand, in which eighty-seven protesters died from suffocation after being detained, bound, and piled into the back of army trucks. The riot started when groups of Muslim youngsters protested against the arrest of several Madrasah pupils and their teacher, whom the authorities accused of preaching radical Islamic ideas.

The incidents marked the end of the peaceful acquiescence of the southern Thais and escalated to several violent incidents, resulting in the killing of many innocent people in the four southern Thai provinces. This has in turn sparked off the ongoing crisis between the Thai-Muslim population and the central government over better economic development in the southern Thai provinces. The separatist movement, led by the new Pattani Union Liberation Organization (PULO), even demanded for secession; a demand which has been the centre of physical clashes between the organization and the military for more than thirty years. The Thai Government viewed its heavy-handed approach towards the riots as a direct response to the separatists' series of killings and arson attacks on government buildings.

The Krue Sae mosque ambush, the Tak Bai incident, and the subsequent iron-fisted policies adopted by the Thaksin administration have led to an escalation of tension between the Thai Government and the Thai-Muslim separatists. It has been argued that separatist activities have long been contained for the last decade and that the Thai-Muslim areas were relatively stable and peaceful.[9] Yet when thirty-six schools in Yala, Narathiwat, and Pattani were set on fire on 1 August 2002, the relatively long peace period in the area was quickly dissolved. The following day, two more schools in Pattani and Songkhla were torched. In February 2003 two gunmen shot a policeman to death in Pattani. One of the gunmen was shot dead, while the other escaped. The government argued that political tensions were systematically created by disgruntled parties whose power bases were affected by the raids against illegal narcotic and prostitution activities. Hence the separatist movements and the Muslim population were blamed for igniting unrest in the provinces. Prime Minister Thaksin earlier insisted that the Muslim youths who were killed in the government crack down were funded by a network of drug traffickers and corrupt politicians. As subsequent evidence proved otherwise, Thaksin changed his tune and labelled the separatist groups as terrorist Islamic groups.[10]

External support and intervention may have come from the neighbouring countries of Malaysia and Indonesia, which are Muslim-dominated countries. The close blood and cultural ties between the southern Muslim Thais and those of Malaysia's northern states have become a thorny issue in Thai–Malaysian relations. In mid-2005 Thai–Malaysian relations were at their lowest ebb when Kuala Lumpur refused to release 131 southern Thais who had sought political refuge in the Malaysian state of Kelantan. The Thai Government blamed the exodus on the separatist groups that created the panic. The Thai authorities also demanded Malaysia's cross-border support for the problems arising from the Thai-Muslim issue. However, the Malaysian Government maintained that it would not be humanitarian to force the refugees to return to Thailand when their lives were threatened by the insurgency.

The southern Thailand conflict has worsened. For the first nine months of 2004, there were more than 600 incidents of unrest, resulting in 250 deaths in the four southern Thai provinces.[11] Accordingly, the Thaksin government declared a state of emergency in the four provinces. In response, the National Reconciliation Commission blamed the government for the series of bloody conflict in the area. The state of emergency, which was criticized by local and overseas liberal groups, gave the administration full control of the area. The inevitable consequences of this conflict were negative economic growth and the undermining of investor confidence. The tourist industry suffered the most. The economy of towns bordering Malaysia, such as Hat Yai, Sungei Kolok, Songkhla, and Yala, suffered due to the lack of incoming Malaysian and Singaporean tourists.

While the Thai Government has justified its tough handling of the separatist attacks on security grounds, critics argue that the underlying grievances of the population in the area should be considered. The government should adopt a face-saving approach by softening its position to regain the trust of the affected population. To win the hearts and minds of Muslims should be the number one priority and the public, Muslims and non-Muslims alike, should be assured necessary steps would be taken to prevent future conflict. Although Madrasah or Islamic schools have been identified as the major source of the radical political ideas, the authorities should avoid taking measures that seek to destroy the credibility of religious leaders and institutions. The iron-fisted approach of the Thaksin government only succeeds in aggravating the conflict. Special but limited autonomy, like that practised in Aceh and Mindanao, is an option that Bangkok ought to consider. Adequate and fair distribution of funding for development purposes should be aggressively pursued in response to the separatists' dissatisfaction and grievances.

The socio-political development in southern Thailand is an unfortunate political development in the region. This is more so given the fact that the governments and separatist movements in other regional conflict areas such as in Aceh seem to have reached some form of political compromise. Likewise, the Philippine Government has also attempted to extend a hand of political conciliation to the separatist movements. Despite Malaysia's mediation in the matter, the solution remains elusive as the number of parties involved and opposing views are too divergent.

The End of Aceh Conflict?

The Aceh conflict has been present since Indonesia gained its independence from the Dutch in 1946. Aceh became the battleground between the Acehnese separatist movements and the government in 1953 when the government refused to consider the rebels' call for greater autonomy and a stronger role for Islam in politics. The conflict ended in 1962 when the

Indonesian Government granted special status to the province of Aceh and absorbed rebel members into the Indonesian Armed Forces (Angkatan Bersenjata Republik Indonesia — Abri). But the conflict resumed when the rebellion led by the newly formed Gerakan Aceh Merdeka (GAM) accused Jakarta of failing to fulfil its promise to grant the province broader autonomy. Formed in 1976, GAM's popularity and support grew with its steady arms supply and well-organized command structure. The Indonesian Government reacted to GAM's rising threat by declaring a Daerah Operasi Militer (Military Operation District or DOM) during the Soeharto era. By the end of the DOM period in 1998, between 1,258 and 2,000 people had been killed, 3,439 tortured, and 39,000 disappeared.[12]

Like the southern Thailand conflict, the Aceh conflict resulted from the government's failure to politically and economically develop the province. The discovery of large petroleum resources in northern Aceh in 1971 resulted in the Indonesian central government's tighter grip over the local economy and politics. Although the province experienced rapid economic growth, the local Acehnese did not directly benefit from the petroleum production. During the peak production of natural gas in 1989–99, only about 5 per cent of the total export revenue remained in Aceh; most of the profits went to the mid-sized enterprises owned mainly by non-indigenous Acehnese.[13]

The Asian *tsunami* of 2004 and its disastrous impact have dramatically changed the socio-political landscape of the conflict. The 26 December 2004 *tsunami* ravaged large parts of Aceh. Despite informal ceasefire agreements between GAM and the government so that aid could be sent to the affected areas in the province, the decades-long violence, armed clashes, and mutual suspicions still lingered. In one instance, unarmed GAM guerillas were ambushed by the Tentera Nasional Indonesia (Indonesian National Army or TNI) when they emerged from the jungle to assist the affected villagers. The clashes, however, did not affect the proposed peace process. This was due to the willingness of both parties to settle some difficult political differences, such as the question of autonomy, the role of the local government, the implementation of *syariah* (Islamic) law, and the future of Aceh's economic development. The *tsunami* may be said to have brought these two traditional enemies to the negotiating table.

As a result, it is hoped that the decades-long conflict would be peacefully resolved. The current administration under Susilo Bambang Yudhoyono appears to be accommodating the rebels' demands. The negotiations between Jakarta and GAM began in June 2001 when a fresh regional autonomy package allowing the province of Aceh to retain 70 per cent of provincial revenues was proposed. The province was renamed Nanggroe Aceh Darusalam (NAD) in

January 2002 and has been allowed to implement the *syariah* law. Although there were several setbacks and intermittent clashes between the TNI and GAM rebels, they have not dissuaded both parties from negotiating under the aegis of the Norwegians. The Helsinki Peace Treaty was signed in August 2005, which eventually ended the hostilities between the two parties and paved the way for accelerated economic development in the province.

The Future of Mindanao Conflict

The Mindanao conflict has also entered a new political chapter. Historically, ethno-religious factors have been responsible for heightening the conflict between the Muslims and the government. The century-long hostility and distrust have long characterized relations between the ruling Christian government and the Muslims in Mindanao. The Jabidah Massacre in 1968 was said to have led to the Moro people's formation of organized fronts and war of liberation. The organized front, initially led by the Moro National Liberation Front (MNLF) and later by Nur Misauri, took major steps to protest against political discrimination, poverty, unequal development of their area as well as the displacement of the Moro communities by the Marcos administration's Christian resettlement programme.

Internal problems within the MNLF led to the formation of the Moro Islamic Liberation Front (MILF) under the leadership of Hashim Selamat. The MILF made demands for full independence as well as the creation of an Islamic state and the institution of Islamic law in Mindanao. Due to an internal problem within the MILF and MNLF, the Abu Sayyaff group was formed. The Abu Sayyaff group, led by Abduragak Abuakar Janalani, does not share the political aspiration of either the MNLF or MILF. Despite the Abu Sayyaff connection to the Al-Qaeda and Jemaah Islamiyah (JI) groups, critics argue that the group has limited political influence *vis-à-vis* the other two Moro political movements.[14]

Political solutions to the Mindanao conflict are problematic. After a series of negotiations, the government agreed to grant Mindanao special autonomy provided the affected provinces in it consented to the proposal through a formal plebiscite. Although the MNLF leadership initially refused to accept the government's proposal of Muslim autonomy, a plebiscite was held in 1989. In the plebiscite four Mindanao provinces — Basilan, Sulu, Tawi-Tawi, and Maguindanao — voted to accept the proffered autonomy and Mindanao was renamed the Autonomous Region of Muslim Mindanao (ARMM). The 1996 Jakarta Accord reaffirmed the ARMM concept when both parties finally agreed to a ceasefire, thereby leading the way to the peace process in the southern Philippines.[15] The Mindanao province of Lanao del Sur and the city of Marawi were incorporated into the ARMM after the treaty. The governance of the ARMM is comprised of the executive, legislative, and judicial branches. Nur Misauri became the first governor of the ARMM and chairman of the Special Zone of Peace and Development Committee (SZOPAD) for the region. Together, the ARMM and SZOPAD would formulate policies and monitor regional economic development.

Despite this promising start corruption, lack of funds for reconstruction, and the government's failure to implement the 1996 agreement fully hampered the role and effectiveness of the ARMM. Nur Misauri was jailed for misappropriation of government funds and a new leadership sympathetic to the central government was appointed. The lopsided allocation of the national budget also resulted in the Christian Mindanao provinces receiving larger amounts than the ARMM. The issue has caused continued political tensions between the ARMM authorities and the central government.

The MILF also engaged in sporadic negotiations with the government. Its demands differed from the MNLF's. The MILF demanded a greater role for *syariah* law. The talks failed several times under the Estrada and Arroyo governments. However, in August 2001 a milestone was achieved when a ceasefire was signed in Kuala Lumpur whereby the MILF agreed to forgo their demand of independence and work together with the government to rebuild Mindanao. In mid-2003 the government–MILF Co-ordinating Committee on the Cessation of Hostilities (CCCH) was set up and international observers from Malaysia, Libya, and Brunei were brought in to monitor the cease-fire. Talks still continue and the Philippine Government has requested the sixty-strong international monitoring team, composed mainly of Malaysian troops, to continue to monitor and safeguard the two-year truce between the MILF and the government.[16] The ceasefire has considerably reduced clashes between government troops and the MILF across Mindanao, and "allowed the holding of Malaysian-brokered peace talks [with an aim to] end the decades-long insurrection that has killed thousands of people and scuttled economic development".[17]

This is a promising outlook, that a settlement could be finally achieved within the current domestic political climate in the Philippines — unlike that of southern Thailand. If either side decides to end the truce, Mindanao would again enter into another cycle of conflict. Due to the number of separatist parties involved, there is much pessimism attached to the possible framework for peace in the area. The conflict may be difficult to resolve as the leaders of the conflicting parties do not always have the support of their subordinates. Several national congressmen with vested self and political interests are the major stumbling blocks to any real amicable solutions. The ARMM administration is beleaguered with corruption and incompetence. Simultaneously, the remnant groups of the MNLF and MILF opposed to the peace process maintain their struggles against the government. In return, the government forces continue to carry out their anti-rebel operations.

GROWING REGIONAL SECURITY CONCERNS AND CHALLENGES

The 11 September 2001 incident was the defining moment for international politics, for it has changed the perception of threat and security arrangements in the region. This new security threat appears to be trans-border in nature and transcends the conventional ideas of identity and nationalism. The Bali and Jakarta's JW Marriot bombings that left hundreds of people dead or injured are grim indicators that the region has become the second front in the U.S.'s global war against terrorism. The Al-Qaeda-linked group, JI, has been blamed for a series of attacks and bombings against Western interests in the region. The links between Al-Qaeda, JI, and local militant Islamic groups render it difficult for enforcement agencies in the affected countries to track the movements of these groups. Although the threats appear to be confined to countries where sizeable Muslim populations are found, such as Indonesia, Malaysia, Singapore, Thailand, and the Philippines, so far only Brunei Darussalam is free from possible attacks. Terrorist threats also appear to have affected other regional security issues, such as the safety of navigation in the Straits of Malacca. Some analysts believe that the Straits of Malacca is a likely and strategic target of regional terrorist groups. If this is true, the consequences would be disastrous for the regional economy and political stability.

Radical Political Islam, Muslim Militancy, and Terrorist Threats

The second Bali bombings in October 2005 shows that the region is still vulnerable to terrorist threats and attacks. Although the blasts were said to have been committed by JI members, there is as yet no proof of JI involvement. The bombings also raise the question of the effectiveness of intelligence networking, sharing, preventive measures, and co-operation among the Southeast Asian countries anxious to counter the threat. To some extent, intelligence gatherings and networking have been successful. The Malaysian and Singapore intelligence communities, for instance, succeeded in foiling attempts by the JI group to blow up the Causeway linking the republic to the southern tip of Malaysia. However, the nature of Indonesia's constitutional laws has resulted in its authorities' limited enforcement capabilities. This, in turn, has curtailed the regional intelligence sharing mechanisms.

Another regional debate is the purported link between Islam and terrorist threats. It cannot be denied that most of the terrorist attacks in the region were conducted by Islamic movements or groups. It must be acknowledged that Islam is traditionally part of Southeast Asia's socio-political transformation. For years Thailand, the Philippines, Malaysia, and Indonesia have confronted radical Islamic movements and separatist movements demanding their own separate identities and independent Islamic states. Some of these groups sought to strike fear in the hearts of the people so as to destabilize the political system. Thailand, the Philippines, and Indonesia have always regarded these movements as terrorist groups. While the activities of these groups were previously confined to each individual country, the activities of the post-11 September terrorist groups have transcended both boundary and political beliefs as well as ethnic and national consideration. Religious fervour seems to have become the guiding principle in uniting radical Muslims sharing the JI's political aspirations.

The world's major powers look on Southeast Asia's security challenges warily. The United States and Australia have labelled the region the second hotbed for counter-terrorism. Chinese and Russian support of the American campaign against terror is more or less tied to their attempts to improve relations with the United States. Interestingly, both China and Russia

> …tried to wield their influence within the multilateral framework of the United Nations, while cooperating with the United States. In reality, however, they were unable to find any opportunity to exercise their influence in the war against terrorism in the face of the US overwhelming military and intelligence capabilities.[18]

Both major powers are saddled with internal issues of terrorism and separatist movements. The U.S. campaign provided the opportunity for these two countries to solve the problems quickly, thus enabling them to concentrate on their economic development and co-operation with the United States.

Thus far, counter-terrorism measures in Southeast Asia have been hampered by domestic political constraints and the limited capabilities of each country's law enforcement agencies. Only Malaysia and Singapore have some kind of preventive laws containing the spread of terrorist threats. The major concern for Southeast Asia is how Indonesia manages the growth of radical political Islam. Indonesia, the world's most populous Muslim county, is a vast archipelago with porous maritime borders, plagued with several separatist movements, a weak central government, corrupt officials, a floundering economy, and a loosely regulated financial system. All these factors make it a fertile ground for terrorist activities.

Individual Southeast Asian countries' response to the threat of religious militancy is varied. Singapore and Malaysia have arrested dozens of Muslim radicals with apparent links to Al-Qaeda. The Philippines has invited American troops to help wipe out the Abu Sayyaff with its suspected Al-Qaeda ties. So far, Indonesia has done little, apart from indicting Abu Bakar Baasyir, the cleric suspected of running an Al-Qaeda-linked terror group, in court.[19] Although Baasyir is currently behind bars, the Susilo administration has made public the news that he may soon be released for good behaviour in prison. The news was greeted with widespread protests from countries affected by the Bali and Jakarta bombings, especially Australia.

Piracy and the Safety of East–West Navigation in Straits of Malacca

The Straits of Malacca is among the world's most important international navigational waterways. This sea lane of communication (SLOC) has invited global concern over the safety of the ships navigating through the Straits. Trade between Europe and the Middle East and East Asian countries, like Japan, South Korea, and China, passes through the Straits. Malaysian, Indonesian, and Singaporean trade is also dependent on the Straits. The Straits of Malacca is not only a waterway for trade navigation, but is also a source of food and livelihood for Malaysia and Indonesia. From the commercial and military angles, the Straits of Malacca is the most important waterway in Southeast Asia. Nearly 600 ships sail through the Straits of Malacca daily, and half of the world's merchant fleets pass through it to the adjacent Singapore, Sunda, and Lombok Straits and the South China Sea. Prevailing threats in the Straits of Malacca encompass a wide spectrum of issues, from minor theft incidents in harbour, armed robberies at sea, environmental pollution, and substantial illegal immigrants to potential maritime disasters.[20] The piracy attacks, however, have lately been escalating, so much so that Malaysia's Chief of Navy, Admiral Dato' Sri Mohd Anwar Hj Mohd Nor argues, "The maritime security challenges in the Straits of Malacca are very complex"; and as such, require special collaborative approach from littoral as well as user states.[21]

Since 1992 the number of piracy cases in the Straits has increased dramatically; it increased by 20 per cent between 2000 and 2003. Nonetheless, the number may be higher than officially reported as some shipping companies do not wish to pay higher insurance premiums. The owner of a ship may refuse to report an incident of piracy for fear that it would invite protracted criminal investigations by the authorities. This would in turn delay the shipment, costing them millions of dollars in losses.

One of the major security concerns is the fact that some of these piracy or high seas armed robbery incidents have been occurring in and around the conflict area of Aceh in northern Sumatra. It is believed that the separatist movements, particularly GAM, are involved in some of the high seas robberies in the northern area of the Straits of Malacca.[22] The increase of piracy incidents has led to suggestions by user states, particularly Japan, South Korea, and the United States, to send their coast guards to the Straits. The suggestion was welcomed by Singapore. Yet other littoral states, namely Indonesia and Malaysia, rejected the idea, arguing that they are capable of protecting the Straits without outside assistance. Given the Straits of Malacca's importance to the East–West trade, the littoral states have responded to the international call to guarantee safe passage for all ships. Since the 11 September attacks on America, these littoral states have been under heavy pressure to ensure that the ships passing through the Straits of Malacca are not targeted by terrorists. User states such as the United States and Japan (through its Maritime Self Defence Force) have stepped up their patrolling surveillance along the Straits so as to protect the shipments of highly sensitive cargoes, such as military equipment.

Piracy also has adverse implications for the littoral states, particularly Malaysia's image in the international community. Many people outside Southeast Asia have the erroneous impression that the Straits of Malacca, most notably in Malaysian territorial waters, has lately become plagued with piracy. It is even believed that Malaysians are the most active maritime pirates in Southeast Asia. This misconception has only encouraged insurance companies to increase the premiums of all cargo shipments to Malaysia and Southeast Asia. Had an investigation been carried out, it would be discovered that Malaysians are rarely involved in piracy. The Malaysian law enforcement agencies have been successful in identifying and apprehending the few who were directly involved in piracy or were members of the piracy syndicates.

The Japanese and South Korean governments have been very active in promoting piracy awareness among regional states through workshops and navy-to-navy talks. It is hoped that such schemes would step up all the trading partners' commitments and efforts in combating piracy. The issue of piracy also has been highlighted at the Western Pacific Naval Symposium (WPNS). The WPNS was attended by the navy chiefs from sixteen countries in the Asia-Pacific region. Maritime piracy was also discussed at the bilateral staff talks between the United States Navy (USN) and Royal Malaysian Navy (RMN), thus marking both countries' concern over the matter.

To effectively deal with the problem of piracy, Southeast Asian countries have to use the multilateral approach to combat piracy and prevent armed robberies on ships.[23] The Malaysian Government, for instance, regards piracy as a crime against humanity as well as a threat to the region's maritime environment. Therefore, it is considered a human security issue. In contrast, the Singapore Government regards piracy as a matter akin to terrorism. For Singapore believes:

> Pirates roaming the waters of Southeast Asia should be regarded as terrorists. There should be no distinction between pirates operating for personal gain and terrorists with political motives. The motives of these attackers are impossible to judge until they are caught. Although we talk about piracy and anti piracy, if there's a crime conducted at sea, sometimes we do not know whether it's pirates or terrorists who occupy the ship so we have to treat them all alike. So in other words if it's piracy we treat it just like terrorism because it is difficult to identify the culprits concerned unless you board the ship.[24]

The recent growing incidence of piracy has raised much concern among ship owners, and could have detrimental effects on the region's economy. Japan, Taiwan, and South Korea are most affected by piracy because 40 per cent of their import and export trade and 80 per cent of their hydrocarbon requirements are transported through the sea lanes in Southeast Asia. In July 2004 the International Maritime Organization introduced the International Ships and Ports Security (ISPS) Code. Under the ISPS port authorities, cargo ships, and oil tankers all over the world have set up communication networks to ensure that all ships are free from terrorist or piracy infiltration.

Based on the present trend and reports, it is believed that piracy activities will continue to remain a threat within the Straits of Malacca. The reasons and problems discussed above suggest that it is almost impossible to achieve the level of zero piracy. Problems in obtaining suitable assets for surveillance and patrolling, as well as confidence-building measures and a united method of co-operation between the respective nations amidst a sensitivity of the neighbouring nations' legal jurisdiction, the involvement of neighbouring maritime agencies in piracy activities, and the sophisticated communication network of the pirates need to be addressed and taken into consideration in combating piracy. It should be noted that modern piracy includes murder, robbery, rape, and other villainous acts at sea; all of which are regarded as anti-humanitarian. It is of the utmost importance that every nation should seriously address piracy and armed robbery against ships by making it a top priority in their security agenda.

OTHER REGIONAL SECURITY CONCERNS AND MECHANISM FOR CO-OPERATION

One of the major debates in the regional security forum revolves around the challenges posed to Southeast Asian security by the rise of China. As one of the most powerful nations in Asia, China's rise has been received with mixed reactions. Its continuing economic expansion for the last two decades has opened up wide opportunities for regional countries in terms of market as well as investment opportunities. Although there were hardly any direct historical confrontations between Southeast Asian countries and mainland China, it is a moot point whether a more confident China would use force to strengthen its political muscles in the regional disputes such as the Taiwan Strait tension and the overlapping claims in the South China Sea.

Southeast Asian countries are more concerned with China's sweeping claims over the Spratly Islands in the South China Sea. The area remains a potential political hot spot in the region. The South China Sea is important to international navigation as it is connected to the Gulf of Siam and the Java Sea, and flows into the most complex series of maritime crossroads in the world. Just as the Mediterranean was the heartland of the classical civilizations of southern Europe, West Asia, and North Africa, the South China Sea is part of Southeast Asia's strategic heartlands.

The disputed area of the Spratlys consists of small islands and atolls believed to be rich in natural resources, especially petroleum and gas. China makes a sweeping claim of ownership on the area known as blue water sea, whereas countries in the region, that is, Taiwan, the Philippines, Vietnam, Brunei Darussalam, and Malaysia, only claim small parts of the area. Since the South China Sea is an important part of the SLOC in the region, China's sweeping claims may affect the solution of the crisis.[25] Some minor clashes between the navies of China and Vietnam have alarmed navigational experts, who fear that these clashes would severely affect the region's SLOC. Jose Almonte furthermore argues:

...ASEAN needs to speak to China with one voice in regards to the South China Sea. China's sweeping claim to the Spratlys is not just about barren islets, some of which disappear at high tide. It is not just about fishing rights, marine resources, or even the hydrocarbon reserves widely believed to lie under the shallow waters of the South China Sea. It is about Southeast Asia's security and survival.[26]

Despite China's preference to negotiate the issue bilaterally, it later agreed to accept ASEAN's code of conduct proposal. The code of conduct may reduce military activities in the area and put less pressure on arriving at an immediate political solution. ASEAN countries, China, and Taiwan, however, still need a long-term solution to resolve the overlapping claims.

At this point, it would be prudent to ask the following questions: Is China's thirst for military modernization in tandem with its increasing economic prowess? Would the rise of China change the regional balance of power configuration? The end of the Cold War has created political and economical opportunities advantageous to China. Politically, China no longer fears Soviet hegemonic design in the Asia-Pacific; and economically, it has placed China in a better position to pursue its economic development and modernization strategies.[27] Furthermore, China's booming economy over the last two decades has also been associated with its increasing expenditure on defence, thereby giving countries in the two sub-regions much fear over the possible resurgence of a militarily powerful China. This fear was further reinforced by the withdrawal of the U.S. military in Subic Bay and "the availability of post Cold War surplus arms at bargain basement price".[28]

The uncertainty and fear of a possible resurgent and militarily powerful China has created an arms race in East and Southeast Asia. Tim Huxley argues that the race has been driven and inspired by the rise of the Chinese military power.[29] Although the People's Liberation Army (PLA) announced that it would cut 500,000 soldiers from its standing army, it has also been devoting major effort to the modernization of aircraft, navy vessels, submarines, and various types of missiles. In 2002 there was an increase of 17.6 per cent in defence expenditure over the previous year.[30] Some analysts argue that the modernization efforts reflect China's concern over Taiwan's remarkable military modernization. It was reported that in the last few years China has procured forty-eight Russian Su-27 fighters, four Kilo-class submarines, and undisclosed numbers of S-300 surface-to-air missiles (SAMs) enough for eight battalions.[31] China was also given licence to produce Su-27 fighters by Russia. China has also successfully tested and launched Dongfeng-31, a strategic missile with a range of 8,000 kilometres. Given this, it is likely that China may purchase thirty Su-30 fighters.

Countries in ASEAN too have started building up militarily. The ASEAN countries' defence modernization programme has been hit hard by the 1997 financial crisis. Despite this, the regional defence budget has increased since 2001. According to Amitav Acharya, the ASEAN countries' defence budget and military modernization can be broken down into four different aspects:[32] First, the defence expenditure of all the ASEAN countries has increased. Among the ASEAN countries, Malaysia and Singapore are the largest spenders (as evinced by a comparative study carried out between 1995 and 2001). Singapore's growth rate of defence expenditure has remained at approximately US$4.5 billion since 1997, whereas Malaysia's defence expenditure reached US$3.1 billion in 2001.[33] Nonetheless, it should be noted that a second

> …more pertinent aspect is the trend in arms procurement, which shows a clear shift towards conventional warfare capabilities in contrast to the counter-insurgent orientation of the past. In this respect, the region's military build-up has focused on developing more capable air and naval forces through acquisition of advanced fighter planes, maritime patrol aircraft, large surface combatants such as corvettes and frigates, missile-equipped patrol craft, and airborne early warning systems.[34]

Indonesia, for instance, plans to purchase US$650 million worth of Russian fighters and helicopters. It is also presently contemplating the procurement of twenty-four reconnaissance planes to monitor and strengthen its maritime air surveillance.[35] Thirdly, strike warfare capabilities of ASEAN countries have been greatly enhanced by the inclusion of advanced precision-guided missiles, including those for aerial combat, aerial ground attack, and air defence roles. Singapore, for instance, is interested in ordering a new generation of aircraft fighters developed by the Lockheed and Boeing companies. Malaysia is contemplating the replacement of its Sukhov jets that it has lost in several air crash incidents. Finally, many regional armed forces have restructured and redesigned their ground forces for rapid deployment missions.

Nonetheless, the military build-up in the region can also be interpreted as each country's normal defence development programme. Some critics argue that China is not a military threat to Southeast Asia.[36] There appears to be a growing confidence in the relationships among ASEAN countries. The proposed ASEAN–China Free Trade Area has been seen as an attempt to reduce possible political tensions between the two parties, thus allowing for some kind of an integrative economic relationship in the future. An interesting development has also taken place in the region. The first Defence Minister Meeting convened in December 2005 in Kuala Lumpur showed that countries in the region were becoming comfortable and better prepared to discuss security and defence issues openly. This is a positive move away from the climate of secrecy during the height of the Cold War period.

Another pertinent question is the role Japan should play in shaping the political strategy for the region. The Plaza accord agreement compelled Japanese manufacturers to look to other Asian countries with lower wage levels and controlled production costs. Japan has been a major investor in Southeast Asia since the early 1990s. Yet, Japan is reluctant to play a bigger role in the region's strategic and political issues. Japan is frequently constrained by the burden of its history; and as such, has tended to move cautiously in shaping Asia's post-Cold War political strategy. At present, it is evident that Japan is more focused on promoting multicultural organizations such as the Asian Development Bank (ADB) where it is one of the largest contributors. Japan positions itself as a bridge between the developing states of Asia and the developed economies of the West. Kenneth Pyle notes that this slowed "evolutionary approach to the political issues of regional order is typical" of Japan's traditional reactive stance in the international system.[37] However, Southeast Asian countries expect a politically active Japan breaking from its cautious post-World War II relations with the United States. Some Asian countries want Japan to lead the region, even though they know that Japan will most likely abide by its traditional cautious approach to the international system. The fear of its historical obstacles means that Japan will "move slowly and with circumspection until the outlines of the future regional order are clear".[38]

Despite all these potential regional hot spots and security concerns, there are several mechanisms for co-operation that may reduce regional tensions. The ASEAN Regional Forum (ARF) shows the Southeast Asian countries' commitment to the promotion of confidence-building measures, the development of preventive diplomacy and that of conflict-resolution mechanism. The ARF has brought together members of ASEAN, Japan, the United States, China, Russia, and the European Union in its fight for Southeast Asian and Asian security. It is an important venue to discuss Asia's security issues and will undoubtedly come to play a large role in securing regional peace and stability. Similarly, there have been attempts within ASEAN to strengthen its regional cohesiveness. The turmoil created by the financial crisis and the Aceh situation is a wake-up call to the ASEAN members that the security environment of the region is changing significantly. There is a growing awareness that the problems of one member country could spill over to other countries. The inclusion of North Korea as the twenty-third member of the ARF highlights the importance of the peninsula issue to ASEAN. The multilateral security co-operation and dialogue would most likely affect the regional security environment positively. Despite its success in developing the first stage process of confidence building, the ARF has yet to move to the second stage, namely that of preventive diplomacy. Although the ministers of the ASEAN countries have agreed to analyse the possibility of moving towards the second stage of the ARF development in the 1997 Ministerial Meeting, there is no consensus on the definition of term; as such, the overlapping concerns of confidence-building measures and preventive diplomacy are ambiguous at best.[39]

CONCLUSION

The future of Southeast Asia in the aftermath of the 11 September attacks hinges on its ability to overcome and manage some of the contentious issues threatening regional stability and peace. Although there are some flash-point areas with the potential to destabilize Southeast Asia, regional organizations such as ASEAN continue to offset these security threats. An effective resolution of the current social-political conflicts in Southeast Asia's affected areas lies in its reconceptualization of economic, social, and political initiatives. The governments involved must work to defuse and not escalate the problems. Furthermore, serious conflict may emerge amid the skyrocketing increase of the oil price. Such a scenario may hamper Southeast Asian governments' initiation of more political and economic reforms. The management of potential conflicts is dependent upon the preparedness and strength of the regional governments. In spite of the gloomy prediction and the potential conflict looming across the region, there is a confidence that this century is indeed an Asia-Pacific one.

NOTES

1. Jim Rolfe, "Security in Southeast Asia: It's not about the War on Terrorism", *Asia-Pacific Security Studies* 1, no. 3 (June 2002): 1–4.
2. J.N. Mak, "The Asia-Pacific Security Order", in *Asia-Pacific in the New World Order*, edited by Anthony McGrew and Christopher Brook (London: Routledge and Open University Press, 1998), pp. 91–92.
3. Ibid., p. 92.
4. Ibid.
5. Amitav Acharya, *Constructing a Security Community in Southeast Asia: ASEAN and the Problem of Regional Order* (London and New York: Routledge, 2001), p. 168.
6. Muthiah Alagappa, *The National Security of the Developing State: Lessons from Thailand* (Massachusetts: Auburn House Publishing Company, 1987), p. 208.

7. *The Star* (Malaysia), 30 April 2004, p. 1.

8. See comments in "Usaha Halang Kemajuan Malayu Thai" [Efforts to thwart Malay-Thai progress], *Utusan Malaysia*, 23 September 2005, p. 10; and "Southern Thailand: Insurgency, Not Jihad", *Executive Summary and Recommendations: Asia Report*, no. 98, 18 May 2005, International Crisis Group, at http://www.crisisgroup.org/home/index.cfm?id=3436&1=1. Accessed on 19 July 2005.

9. "Malaysia-Thai Border Bother", *Asian Defense Journal*, June 2004, p. 5.

10. See John Aglionby's analysis on the crisis in Thailand, *The Guardian* (UK), 5 June 2004.

11. "Signs of Spreading Unrest", *The Star* (Malaysia), 5 April 2005, p. 4.

12. See Human Rights Watch, *Indonesia: The War in Aceh* 13, no. 4 (August 2001):8; Amnesty International, *"Shock Therapy", Restoring Order in Aceh, 1989–1993*, August 1993, p. 8; and Kristen E. Schulze, *The Free Aceh Merdeka (GAM): Anatomy of a Separatist Organization* (Washington, D.C.: East-West Center, 2004), p. 5.

13. Sylvia Tiwon, "From Heroes to Rebels", *Inside Indonesia*, no. 62 (April–June 1999), at http://www.insideindonesia.org/edit62/sylvia1.htm. Accessed on 24 March 2005.

14. See Zachary Abuza, "Tentacles of Terror: Al-Qaeda's Southeast Asian Network", *Contemporary Southeast Asia* 24, no. 3 (December 2002): 427–65; and Taha Basman, "MILF and Abu Sayyaf Group", in *Militant Islamic Movements in Indonesia and Southeast Asia*, edited by S. Yunanto et al. (Jakarta: The Ridep Institute and Friedrich Ebert Stiftung, 2003), pp. 251–61.

15. There were several peace accords between the MNLF and the government, such as the 1976 Tripoli Agreement sponsored by the Organization of Islamic Conference (OIC) and the ceasefire agreements of 1986 and 1987. Those agreements suffered setbacks when both parties failed to abide by the terms of the ceasefires.

16. *New Straits Times* (Malaysia), 15 August 2005, p. 30.

17. Ibid.

18. *East Asia Strategic Review 2003* (Tokyo: National Institute for Defense Studies, 2003), p. 48.

19. Hambali, one of the masterminds of the JI activities in the region, was captured by the Thai authorities and handed over to the custody of the United States. It is believed that Hambali is now at the Guantanamo Bay detention centre in Cuba. Another major mastermind of the JI activities, Azhari Karim, believed to be the most dangerous man in the region, is still at large.

20. Mohd Anwar Hj Mohd Nor, "Managing Security of the Straits of Malacca: The Royal Malaysian Navy's Perspective" (Paper presented at the international conference on The Straits of Malacca: Building a Comprehensive Security Environment, jointly organized by the Maritime Institute of Malaysia [MIMA], Universiti Utara Malaysia [UUM], and Universiti Putra Malaysia [UPM], Kuala Lumpur, 11–13 October 2004).

21. Ibid.

22. T. Selva, "Avoid Acheh coast, ships told", *The Star* (Malaysia), 16 February 2004, p. 28.
23. See also Mak Joon Nam and B.A. Hamzah, *The External Maritime Dimension of ASEAN Security* (Kuala Lumpur: MIMA, 1999).
24. "Pirates must be regarded as terrorists, says Singapore", *New Straits Times* (Malaysia), 22 November 2003, p. B23.
25. Chen Hurng-Yu, "The PRC's South China Sea Policy and Strategies of Occupation in the Paracel and Spratly Islands", *Issues and Studies* 36, no. 4 (July/ August 2000): 95–131.
26. Jose T. Almonte, "ASEAN Must Speak with One Voice on the South China Sea", *PacNet*, no. 11, 17 March 2000, at http://www.nyu.edu/globalbeat/asia/ Pacnet031700.html. Accessed on 1 September 2005.
27. Javed Maswod, "The Rise of Asia-Pacific", in *Asia-Pacific in the New World Order*, edited by Anthony McGrew and Christopher Brook (London: Routledge and Open University Press, 1998), p. 62.
28. Mak, op. cit., p. 94.
29. Tim Huxley, "South-east Asia's Arms Race: Some Notes on Recent Developments", *Arms Control* 11, no. 1 (May 1990): 69–76.
30. *East Asia Strategic Review 2003*, p. 185.
31. *East Asia Strategic Review 2001* (Tokyo: National Institute for Defense Studies, 2001), pp. 195–96.
32. Acharya, op. cit., pp. 136–41.
33. *East Asia Strategic Review 2003*, p. 227.
34. Ibid., p.137.
35. Ibid.
36. Du Yanling, "Security Cooperation in Asia: Favourable Condition and Adverse Factors", in *Building New Asia*, edited by Mahavir Singh (New Delhi: Shipra Publications, 2005), pp. 18–32.
37. Kenneth Pyle, "Restructuring Foreign and Defence Policy: Japan", in *Asia-Pacific in the New World Order*, edited by Anthony McGrew and Christopher Brook (London: Routledge and Open University Press, 1998), p. 62.
38. Ibid., pp. 135–36.
39. *East Asia Strategic Review 2004* (Tokyo: National Institute for Defense Studies, 2004), p. 90.

3

Changing Security Environments in Northeast Asia: A Korean View

Seo-Hang Lee

GEOPOLITICAL FEATURES OF NORTHEAST ASIA

Although the countries constituting Northeast Asia are few, the region's security environment is very complicated. The following geopolitical elements complicate the security situation of the region:[1]

- The existence of the world's only remaining divided state, North and South Korea;

- The existence of two states with nuclear capabilities — China and Russia;

- The military presence of another state with nuclear capabilities, the United States — which is allied to the Republic of Korea (hereafter cited as Korea or ROK) and Japan;

- The absence of official bilateral relations between North Korea and the United States, as well as between North Korea and Japan; and

- The presence of two vast semi-enclosed seas, causing various maritime disputes, including territorial ones.

With these geopolitical elements, security in the Northeast Asian region has long been characterized by the following three features.

First, there is a deep-rooted distrust and rivalry arising from the states' historical experiences with each other. This is reflected in the volatile relations between the two sets of major powers, namely China and Japan, and China and the United States.

Second, the region's political survival is not only dependent on each state's international autonomy and territorial integrity, but also the protection of its existing political system and survival of its incumbent government. This is one of the core security concerns for some of the states in the region, particularly North Korea and Taiwan.

Third, the formation of alliance and alignment has been a key security strategy for most of the Northeast Asian states. The security order created during the Cold War era was built on a complete set of bilateral alliances, with the United States as a maritime power and, less stably, the Soviet Union as a continental power. Given the strategic alliance emphasis to security, the area had been largely bipolar, and there were little horizontal linkages between alliance partners. After the collapse of the Soviet Union, China filled the power vacuum and the post-Cold War bipolar regional structure is now characterized by the Chinese dominance of mainland Northeast Asia and U.S. dominance of maritime Northeast Asia.[2]

Over the past few years, the security environment of Northeast Asia has been relatively stable, with the exception of the North Korean nuclear issue. In particular, the end of the Cold War has generally reduced international tensions across the region by improving bilateral relationships among regional countries. The preoccupation of virtually all countries in the region with accelerating economic development and enhancing their economic competitiveness has encouraged them to promote co-operative commercial relations with their neighbours, thereby contributing to a reduction of tensions. As a result, trade among Northeast Asian countries has significantly increased in recent years, and intra-regional interdependence is improving annually. In particular, China's accession to the World Trade Organization (WTO), which was finalized in November 2001, has accelerated the Chinese economy's expansion and its incorporation into the global and regional markets. Consequently, this has spurred an increase in the intra-regional trade volume and greater economic interdependence among the countries in the region.

In 2002 China became the biggest importer to Japan over the United States. Similarly, Japan's exports to China exceeded half of those to the United States. Also, there was rapid growth in trade relations between China and Korea. In 2004 China began to rank first in Korean foreign trade with about

US$79 billion, surpassing the latter's amount with the United States. Such increases in intra-regional trade volume along with strengthened economic interdependence are expected to contribute to a stable security environment in the region.[3]

However, conflicts and challenges likely to affect regional peace and security remain, some of which can be attributed to the legacy of the Cold War. These include various sources of conventional security issues, which will be explored in the next section. There is also a growing agenda of non-conventional security issues in the region. While these issues do not involve direct military deployment, they could give rise to the threat or use of force. These include the management of natural resources; the protection of the environment, in particular, trans-border air and marine pollution; the regulation of refugees; and the prevention of international criminal activities such as terrorism, piracy, human smuggling, drug trafficking, and cyber crime. In particular, the United States' experience in the aftermath of the 11 September 2001 terrorist attacks has provided the impetus for all Northeast Asian countries to renew their understanding of non-conventional security threats and trans-national crimes such as terrorism so that they will make the conceptualization of appropriate countermeasures a top security priority.

CURRENT SECURITY CHALLENGES IN NORTHEAST ASIA: SOME NEGATIVE DEVELOPMENTS

With its unique geopolitical features, Northeast Asia is currently facing the following four security challenges most likely to affect regional peace and stability.

First, there is a rise of nationalism or nationalistic sentiments in the region. By definition, nationalism seeks to identify a behavioural entity — the nation — and thereafter to pursue certain political and cultural goals on behalf of it.[4] Over the past few years, this feature of nationalism has had a larger presence in the region, surfacing as a primary element of interstate friction. Propped up by economic dynamism, Northeast Asia has been on the road to becoming one of the world's central strategic pillars since the beginning of the post-Cold War era. However, regional powers' intention to expand their spheres of influence, fanned by nationalism, threatens to weaken regional security. Nationalist forces are deeply rooted in Chinese and Japanese societies, the two major powers in the region. These factions, with their chauvinistic nature, do not conceal their ambition to achieve Asian and global hegemony by building a prosperous nation and a powerful army. Their beliefs have won them wider support bases at home in recent years. As a result, the two countries' foreign policies have taken on defiant and hegemony-oriented tones.

In China's case, Beijing has recently attempted to remap its ethnic frontiers by including Korea's ancient Goguryeo Kingdom (37 B.C.–668 A.D.) in its annals under the Northeast Project to support China's centrality and omnipresence in the greater region. The major purpose of the project was to make the history of all the nation's minority races its own. In Japan's case, the recent attempt to glorify its imperialism in some of its history textbooks, the Prime Minister's and some conservative politicians' regular visit to the Yasukuni Shrine, and a few conservative politicians' remarks justifying Tokyo's imperialism are some examples of the very problematic issue of nationalism in Northeast Asia. The rise of nationalism in the region has joined hands with traditional and non-traditional seeds of instability such as maritime territorial disputes and fierce competition for energy development. It is highly likely, then, that nationalism will bring on the synergy effect of adding to the uncertainties and fluidity prevalent in the region.

The second notable security challenge in Northeast Asia in recent years is the phenomenon of arms build-up throughout the region. Over the past decade, the region's military spending and arms procurement have grown rapidly (for instance, China's military budget has been increasing at a double-digit rate for seventeen consecutive years),[5] and its defence industries have expanded. Northeast Asian governments and most academics argue that the regional states have simply "modernized" their armed forces, implying mere upgrading or replacement of existing equipment. But many have in fact developed new capabilities, going far beyond simple modernization by seeking to increase mobility, precision, and the ability to project power.

The emphasis of the regional arms build-up has been given to conventional weapons, in particular air forces and naval capabilities. For instance, China has accelerated the development of a new air force system, upgrading its own weapons, and at the same time importing Russian combat fighters such as the Su-30MKK aircraft. In China special attention has been also given to naval capabilities, as the country is working hard to have a so-called "blue-water navy", that is, a navy capable of operating far out at sea.[6]

In strengthening air force and naval capabilities, Japan is no exception. Since the early 1990s Japan has gradually improved its capability to project power overseas, particularly developing and acquiring aerial refuellers, Osumi-class transport vessels, and Aegis-class destroyers. Japan has been allegedly moving to build its first aircraft carriers since the end of World War II in a stealthy expansion of its military strike potential.[7]

In Northeast Asia there has also been a significant non-conventional dimension to military programmes. This has involved developing and deploying weapons of mass destruction and associated delivery systems — namely ballistic missiles. For example, China has recently rushed production of short-range ballistic missiles, mainly "to fight and win short-duration, high-intensity conflicts" over Taiwan, according to a report issued by the U.S. Defense Department in July 2005.[8]

Why are regional states engaging in arms build-up? The motivations behind the arms build-up in Northeast Asia today are complex and vary according to country. The single most important cause of the arms build-up in the region is the perception of strategic uncertainty in Northeast Asia characterized by rapid and wrenching political change, and where the long-term commitment of the United States seems problematic. Confronting a highly uncertain strategic future, regional states are, prudently in their view, planning for the worst.

The third noticeable security concern in Northeast Asia is the emergence of competition (or checks and balances) among the four major powers, namely China, Japan, Russia, and the United States. Since the end of the Cold War, the four major powers have made sustained efforts at both the bilateral and multilateral levels to enhance co-operation and exchanges across a broad spectrum of areas, including counter-terrorism, counter-proliferation, and economics. Despite these endeavours, the United States' and Japan's shared vigilance against the other two's (China in particular) rapidly increasing national power and China's sensitive reaction to this are stirring tensions in their respective bilateral relations.

For instance, in February 2005 the United States and Japan enhanced their military alliance by adopting a joint statement on a new set of common security objectives aimed at containing China's military power in the region. For the first time in their decades-old alliance, the two countries referred to Taiwan as the site of their mutual security concern. China made a firm response to this statement by saying that it "resolutely opposes the United States and Japan in issuing any bilateral document concerning China's Taiwan, which meddles in the internal affairs of China, and hurts China's sovereignty".[9] In July 2005 China adopted a joint declaration on the twenty-first century world order with Russia, and engaged in a joint military exercise with Russia in August in the Yellow Sea basin. Although no country was identified or targeted by name in the declaration and the exercise, China's activities are to some extent to counter the United States' and Japan's move to contain China. In the near future the competition among the four major powers will be more visible and is likely to intensify. Moreover, this rise of check and balance between the United States and Japan on the one hand and China and Russia on the other has the potential to exacerbate the structural instability in the region.

The last, but not least, security challenge in Northeast Asia today is the North Korean nuclear issue. Pyongyang's drive to become an indigenous nuclear power represents a threat not only to the security of the Northeast Asian region, but also to the system that has been painstakingly developed to limit the proliferation of nuclear weapons in the world.

Since October 2002, when the second nuclear crisis started, North Korea has taken a series of alarming steps, including the withdrawal from the Nuclear Non-proliferation Treaty (NPT) in January 2003 and the announcement of possession of nuclear weapons in February 2005. Pyongyang's stated objectives were to obtain U.S. recognition of North Korea's sovereignty, security assurances, and abandonment of Washington's hostile policy. To resolve the North Korean nuclear issue, the Six-Party Talks — involving the two Koreas, the United States, China, Japan, and Russia — are currently under way. So far, four rounds of talks have been held and on 19 September 2005, an agreement was reached in Beijing for the first time in more than two years, for North Korea to abandon all its nuclear activities and dismantle its existing nuclear weapons, in return for energy supplies and guarantees that the United States and its allies would not attack it.[10]

However, the agreement had no timetable for Pyongyang to abandon its nuclear programme and the North Korean nuclear issue is an integral part of a bigger puzzle, namely the North Korean problem as a whole. This problem will only be resolved when North Korea emerges from its self-imposed isolation and becomes interdependent with other countries in the region. This perhaps constitutes the single most critical security challenge for the future of Northeast Asia. In other words, the resolution of Pyongyang's nuclear issue, the fate of North Korea, and the future of Northeast Asian security are all tied together. And the thorniest point remains Pyongyang's nuclear issue.[11]

EFFORTS TO STABILIZE NORTHEAST ASIA

With the above-mentioned security challenges in Northeast Asia, the region is often described as "All Not Quiet on the Eastern Front".[12] Northeast Asia is not only the nucleus for the Asia-Pacific's dynamic economic growth process, but also a region of intractable geopolitical conflicts, deep-seated animosities, and dangerous strategic calculus. How can we, then, overcome these various security challenges and stabilize the region?

Over the last decade a number of significant multilateral efforts have emerged in Northeast Asia to stabilize the region. These include, at the official level, the Four-Party Talks; the Korean Peninsula Energy Development

Organization; the informal summit meeting among Japan, China, and Korea in the ASEAN plus Three (APT) setting; and most recently the Six-Party Talks to resolve the North Korean nuclear issue.

On the Track II level the Northeast Asia Co-operation Dialogue (NEACD), the North Pacific Working Group of the Council for Security Co-operation in the Asia-Pacific (CSCAP), and other groups have also contributed to enhancing mutual understanding. As of April 2005 the NEACD has met sixteen times since 1993 and has developed a set of Principles of Co-operation in Northeast Asia. In addition, more frequent summit and high-level meetings have strengthened bilateral relations; particularly significant was the summit meeting between the leaders of North and South Korea in June 2000. Moreover, all Northeast Asian countries are now members of the ASEAN Regional Forum (ARF), whose primary objectives are to promote confidence-building, develop preventive diplomacy, and elaborate approaches to conflict resolution in the region.

These positive developments in regional multilateral security dialogue have provided good experiences for all the participating countries. However, in none of them — except the recently established Six-Party Talks — did officials from all six countries in Northeast Asia (China, Japan, Russia, the United States, and the two Koreas) sit down together and discuss ways to increase understanding and build confidence.

There is both a foundation and a need for such discussions. Although the objective of the Six-Party Talks is limited to the North Korean nuclear issue, a new pattern was set up in Northeast Asia. Therefore, once progress has been made in resolving the North Korean nuclear issue, the Six-Party Talks could serve as a Northeast Asian multilateral security framework, in which further measures to stabilize the region can be explored. Simply put, the resolution of the North Korean nuclear issue will determine whether the Six-Party Talks will undergo a makeover into a multilateral security organization.

CONCLUSIONS

The security trend in Northeast Asia today is mixed. On the one hand, there is a positive movement as reflected in an increased intra-regional economic interdependence. On the other hand, conflicts stemming from the Cold War legacy may likely continue to affect regional peace and stability. The post-Cold War era in the region therefore represents a profound transition.

At present, the Six-Party Talks are determining whether the North Korean nuclear problem can be expeditiously resolved. An agreement was reached in Beijing in September 2004 for North Korea to abandon all its nuclear activities in return for energy supplies. However, the agreement had no concrete timetable for Pyongyang to abandon its nuclear programme. This problem will only be resolved when North Korea emerges from its self-imposed isolation and becomes interdependent with other countries in the region. If the Six-Party Talks is able to yield tangible outcomes for a peaceful resolution of the North Korean nuclear issue, it could develop into a multilateral security dialogue forum capable of tackling Northeast Asia's broader security and confidence-building issues.

NOTES

1. For more details on the geopolitical features of Northeast Asia, see Robert Ross, "The Geography of the Peace: East Asia in the Twenty-First Century", *International Security* 23 (Spring 1999): 81–118; and Thomas J. Christensen, "China, the U.S.–Japan Alliance, and the Security Dilemma in East Asia", *International Security* 23 (Spring 1999): 49–80.

2. Ross, op. cit., p. 84.

3. Currently, the intra-regional trade of the major Northeast Asian economies (China, Japan, Korea, Taiwan, and Hong Kong) constitutes more than 35 per cent of their total trade. In the process regional trade has changed from a vertical to a horizontal structure (exchanging parts and finished products) or to that of intra-firm and intra-industry trade. This indicates that production networks have been created within Northeast Asia. Due to the export-led growth of Northeast Asian economies, the freight volumes handled by the region's major ports have been increasing dramatically. A survey showed that out of the world's ten largest container-handling ports in 2003, the top five were in Northeast Asia. They included, among others, Hong Kong, Busan, and Shanghai.

4. Graham Evans and Jeffrey Newnham, *Dictionary of International Relations* (New York: Penguin Books, 1998), p. 346.

5. *International Herald Tribune*, 3 August 2005, p. 1.

6. Ibid., p. 4.

7. *The Times*, 8 August 2003, p. 17.

8. *International Herald Tribune*, 21 July 2005, p. 3.

9. *New York Times*, 21 February 2005.

10. *International Herald Tribune*, 20 September 2005.

11. Francois Godement, "Northeast Asia: Time to Rethink?" *Disarmament Forum*, no. 2 (2005), p. 11.

12. James R. Lilley, "All Not Quiet on the Eastern Front", *Wall Street Journal*, 13 April 2005.

PART II

Non-Traditional Security Threats

4

Strengthening ASEAN–Korea Co-operation in Non-Traditional Security Issues

Carolina G. Hernandez

INTRODUCTION

Within the ASEAN plus Three process, the ASEAN–South Korea economic, functional, and political relationships remain the weakest *vis-à-vis* those of ASEAN, China, and Japan. Both China and Japan have forged their own free trade agreements/comprehensive economic co-operation packages with ASEAN. In contrast, despite an agreement to start free merchandise trade starting in 2006 having been reached, South Korea has yet to complete ongoing talks with ASEAN on free cross-border investment and trade in services.[1]

Political relations between ASEAN and China are also at an all-time high, particularly with the much-diminished Chinese assertiveness on the South China Sea issue. This has been capped by the conclusion of the ASEAN–China Declaration on the Conduct of Parties in the South China Sea in Phnom Penh on 2 November 2002. Furthermore, Japan has sustained its long history of mutually beneficial economic and political co-operation with ASEAN when it marked the thirtieth year of bilateral relations in 2003. On the other hand, South Korea and ASEAN agreed in 2000 to include an exchange of views on political and security issues in the region in their dialogue.

The gap between ASEAN's relationship with China and Japan on the one hand and South Korea on the other is even more notable in the security field. This is despite the fact that security issues are included in their dialogues. Although ASEAN is concerned about the proliferation of nuclear weapons on the Korean Peninsula, this issue is not as great a priority as the post-11 September 2001 anti-terrorism endeavours. This overarching concern with terrorism is surprising given that the ASEAN states do not conform to the overweening priority given by the United States' predominantly military response to international terrorism. Nevertheless, ASEAN states have since stepped up their security co-operation with enhanced information and intelligence sharing, among other measures, in order to combat terrorism.

Sino–ASEAN security co-operation, most notably Sino–Filipino security co-operation, has been stepped up in recent years. Given that the Philippines is the oldest U.S. ally in the region, this is not surprising. The Beijing and Manila military and defence establishments have agreed on a number of confidence-building measures, and China has agreed to provide security assistance to the Philippine military. The perceived growing security co-operation between the two countries has created further difficulties in the Philippine–American relationship following the premature pull-out of the Philippine humanitarian contingent from Iraq in 2004. Washington felt slighted by these two developments for understandable strategic reasons.

On the other hand, Japan has sustained a series of workshops and symposiums on security co-operation with ASEAN since 2003. These include workshops on maritime safety and security, military modernization and weapons of mass destruction (WMD), international terrorism, transnational crime, environmental and natural disasters, peace making, peace keeping, peace building, and post-conflict reconstruction, as well as institutional arrangements to enhance security co-operation. It has also conducted coast guard capacity-building programmes with a number of ASEAN states so as to promote regional maritime safety and security.

Similarly, South Korea signed an anti-terrorism co-operation pact with its ASEAN dialogue partners in July 2005. In so doing, it has enhanced the South Korean and ASEAN security co-operation.

In all of these ASEAN plus Three developments, South Korean participation continues to lag behind, especially in security co-operation and non-traditional security (NTS) issues where co-operation among new parties appears to have been stepped up in recent years (for example, in combating pandemic diseases, including HIV/AIDS, Severe Acute Respiratory Syndrome [SARS], and avian flu). However, lately it has joined ASEAN and its other dialogue partners in an anti-terrorism co-operation agreement. If the East Asia community-building project is to be successful, all three sets of bilateral relations must undergo parallel developments. The ASEAN–South Korean relationship is as critical to this project as the two other sets of bilateral relationships, as NTS issues have increasingly become important matters. As a consequence of the erosion of national borders wrought by increasing interdependence, the ICT revolution, and other forces of globalization, regional security must be recognized as a seamless web whose parts are inseparable. Hence, East Asian security is dependent on all the parties forging security relationships.

Moreover, ASEAN and South Korea are the weakest of the four players within the ASEAN plus Three process. Despite ASEAN's many advantages in its relations with China and Japan, stronger regional actors are constantly seeking closer relations with individual ASEAN states. While ASEAN continues to play an important swing role in balancing the power between the two major Northeast Asian nations, it is still vulnerable to the two major economies of China and Japan, with which ASEAN states are interdependent. ASEAN states are so dependent on China and Japan that they have continued to benefit from their productive relations with these two countries after the Asian financial crisis of 1997. ASEAN also needs South Korea if it is to maintain its role as an independent player in regional politics.

South Korea would be vulnerable if it were left to deal with both China and Japan on its own. Any Korean initiative requiring regional support, beyond the strictly Korean Peninsula issues — such as the East Asia community envisaged by the East Asia Vision Group (EAVG) and the East Asia Study Group (EASG) — has to occur with ASEAN co-operation. This was the case in the Korean initiative to convene members of the Experts and Eminent Persons Groups (EEPGs) of the ASEAN Regional Forum (ARF) in the first quarter of 2005. This was supported by the ARF EEPGs. In addition, domestic dynamics in South Korea in recent years, such as the generational change, new nationalism, and increased role of China in the Korean Peninsula's security problems, has had some impacts on Seoul's alliance with the United States. As South Korea gravitates towards Beijing, the Chinese Government has reassessed its strategic value of South Korea.

Having laid the background to ASEAN–South Korean relations, this chapter advocates the strengthening of ASEAN–South Korea relations in the NTS realm. Most of the NTS issues are transnational issues affecting all countries and do not require the forging of difficult military alliances. Therefore, these NTS issues are common challenges requiring efforts beyond that of military and defence co-operation; and as such, ought to be easier to undertake. However, this could be a challenge if the parties involved have markedly different perceptions as to the nature of the security challenges facing them or if there is a wide disparity in their interpretation of the danger posed by a specific security threat.

The chapter discusses the NTS issues facing East Asia, the differences in ASEAN and South Korean perspectives surrounding these security issues, and makes a case for enhancing bilateral co-operation in some of these issues. Among these issues are various forms of transnational crime, global terrorism, pandemic diseases, the energy crisis, and environmental degradation affecting ASEAN and South Korea in different ways. These NTS issues then could be important challenges to the strengthening of their relationship.

NON-TRADITIONAL SECURITY ISSUES IN EAST ASIA

Transnational Crime

Transnational crime[2] is one of the most important NTS challenges presently facing East Asia and the rest of the world. Although various regional and international efforts have been exerted to combat different forms of transnational crime (including a United Nations convention and three protocols on transnational crime), there is no single definition of transnational crime. Experts say that transnational crime involves the criminal act of people or objects crossing any geographical border; and the international recognition that such an act constitutes a crime. It takes many forms, such as the illegal trafficking of drugs, human beings, small arms and light weapons, piracy, illegal immigration, money laundering, and cyberspace crime.

There are currently several transnational crimes with the potential to seriously affect East Asian regional security. These are illegal trafficking in drugs, human beings, especially women and children, small arms and light weapons; and piracy. Studies on transnational crime indicate that these forms of crime are often inter-related. Illegal traffickers in drugs use small arms to secure their production sites and distribution routes. These arms are usually purchased from the black market. Pirates use illegally procured arms; so do those engaging in the illegal trafficking of human beings. They also tend to resort to document fraud and money laundering in the pursuit of their illegal activities.

Porous national borders, inadequate legal instruments, weak law enforcement regimes, collusion between transnational criminal organizations and law enforcement officers, superiority of criminal over law enforcement resources, and inadequate regional and international co-operation are the factors often associated with the spread of transnational crime. Thus, collective co-operative regional and global responses are instrumental to drastically reducing or eradicating transnational crime. Regardless of a state's strength and determination, it would not be able to deter and defeat transnational crime without the co-operation of others.

Illegal Traffic in Drugs

Illegal drug trafficking has already grown to a US$400-billion-a-year industry worldwide. This represents 8 per cent of total world exports in 1995. Some 140 million people, or 2.5 per cent of the world's population, smoke marijuana and hashish, 13 million use cocaine, 8 million use heroin, and 30 million use stimulants like amphetamine.[3]

Illicit drug trafficking in our region has also risen. As Southeast Asia is the home of opium production and trafficking, it has also become a producer and transshipment point for synthetic drugs such as "ice" and "Ecstasy". Porous borders, collusion between government agents and transnational criminal syndicates, as well as globalization have facilitated the region's growth of the illegal drugs problem (and other transnational crimes such as the trafficking in women and children).

While China serves as a key destination and transshipment point for heroin produced in Myanmar, Thailand remains a principal transit corridor and market. Although heroin trafficking through Thailand has dropped in recent years due to tighter border patrols, Laos, Vietnam, and Cambodia have emerged as secondary transit zones and markets. Southeast Asian heroin and opium are smuggled to Australia through Laos, Vietnam, and Cambodia. Indonesia, Malaysia, and Singapore have emerged as markets and transit routes for heroin bound for the European, Australian, and U.S. markets.[4]

The campaign against illicit drugs, like the fight against global terrorism, has negatively impacted some states' progress in their rules of law, due process, human rights implementation, and democratization. In Thailand, for example, its National Human Rights Commission reported in 2005 that some 2,500 people were killed through summary execution since January 2004 in the country's campaign against illicit drugs. This represents a retreat in the country's reform of its rule of law, due process, human rights, and democracy.

Illegal drug trafficking is a threat to the security of people and states. It produces the following results, among others: (1) illicit drugs use has resulted in the physical and mental decay of users; (2) it has been associated with the increase in heinous crimes in various societies; (3) profits from their illicit traffic are also known to have funded other forms of transnational crime such as illegal trafficking in human beings and small arms, as well as money laundering; (4) it has corrupted the military, police, other law enforcement agents, and government officials, especially in developing countries, further weakening state capacity; and (5) it has undermined the capacity of young people who become victims of drug use, thereby preventing them from becoming productive members of their society and responsible parents for the future generation.

Illegal Trafficking in Human Beings

The illegal trafficking in human beings is increasingly centred around China. A number of ASEAN countries are critical transshipment points for the illegal trafficking of human beings. It was estimated that approximately 800,000 to 900,000 people are trafficked annually across international borders worldwide. Between 18,000 and 20,000 of them are trafficked into the United States. They are trafficked into forced labour and for sexual exploitation and the sale of human organs. This illicit trade, according to the United Nations, generates US$7 to US$10 billion annually for traffickers.

The dynamism inherent in these illegal activities is indicated in U.S. reports of individual countries' compliance with minimum standards for the elimination of trafficking. According to the degree of compliance with these minimum standards established by the United States' Trafficking Victims Protection Act of October 2000, Tier One refers to countries whose governments fully comply with these minimum standards, Tier Two represents those governments that do not fully comply but are making significant efforts to bring themselves into compliance with them, and Tier Three refers to governments that do not fully comply with them and are not making significant efforts to do so. Eight ASEAN countries were put in Tier Two, while Myanmar remained in Tier Three in 2003.[5] Singapore was not listed at all in any of the three tiers in 2003. However, the June 2005 report added Cambodia to Tier Three alongside Myanmar, and Singapore to Tier Two. While the Philippines remained in Tier Two, the Trafficking Victims Protection Act has put it on the Watch List. Indonesia was the only ASEAN state cited as having its workers trafficked to South Korea, among other destination countries.[6]

According to United Nations Development Fund for Women (UNIFEM), there are no reliable estimates of the number of women trafficked; and there are no records of these women's origin and destination. In Thailand the only reliable estimates are those related to prostitution. In 1995 the Thai Public Health Ministry estimated that there were 81,384 Thai commercial sex workers, but the Police Department's estimate was 500,000, based on the number of registered entertainment places. Non-governmental organizations working on children's rights issues estimate that the number of child prostitutes ranges between 200,000 (ECPAT 1994) and 800,000 (Centre for Protection of Children's Rights, 1989). These estimates include Thai, Myanmar, Chinese, Laotian, and Cambodian children and also those who have been trafficked into Thailand's sex industry.[7]

In the trafficking of women and children, countries in the region serve as the points of origin, transshipment points, or destination areas. Trafficked women and children into the entertainment and sex industries, sweatshops, or as domestic help mostly come from Cambodia, China, Indonesia, Laos, Malaysia, Myanmar, the Philippines, Thailand, and Vietnam. Cambodia, Malaysia, and Thailand are the points of origin, transshipment, and destination countries, while Brunei, Japan, and Singapore serve as destination countries. If the number of pages on child trafficking statistics is any guide to the extent of the participation of ASEAN countries in this illicit trade, Thailand tops them all (that is, over four pages), followed by the Philippines and Vietnam (two pages each).[8]

The establishment of the Council on Security Cooperation in the Asia-Pacific (CSCAP) Study Group on Human Trafficking demonstrates that this is indeed a regional problem. This study group constantly sends its reports on the human trafficking problem to governments in the region through the ARF. It also advocates that governments ought to respond to human trafficking by making regional arrangements and passing legislation, emphasizing capacity building for agencies dealing with this crime type, as well as promoting national public awareness initiatives, providing victim support/protection, and identifying convergence between crime types.[9]

Smuggling of Small Arms and Light Weapons

Small arms include self-loading pistols, revolvers, rifles, carbines, submachine guns, assault rifles, and light machine guns. Light weapons, on the other hand, refer to heavy machine guns, portable anti-aircraft weapons, anti-tank weapons, recoilless rifles, grenade-launchers, and mortars of a calibre of less than 100 millimetres. These weapons not only form the foundation of any organized military force; they are also essential for crime syndicates, drug traffickers, insurgent groups, and terrorists.[10]

While there are no concrete figures on the number of small arms and light weapons smuggled into Southeast Asia, it is well known that the prevalence of intra-state conflicts in mainland Southeast Asia feeds the demand for these weapons. These weapons are not newly produced ones, but are from exist-ing stockpiles. Vietnam and Cambodia inherited about two million firearms and 150,000 tons of ammunition following the U.S. withdrawal in 1975. Even after a government crackdown, experts believe that there are still some 500,000 to one million military-style weapons circulating in Cambodia alone. The Philippines has between 600,000 and 700,000 guns registered with the Philippine National Police (PNP), while estimates of unregistered arms in circulation vary from 270,000 to 600,000. A report of the Philippine Center on Transnational Crime puts the figure closer to 350,000 — divided between 189,766 unregistered firearms and 157,860 loose firearms.[11]

These weapons reach the illicit arms market through a "leak", where weapons are sold or stolen from legitimately held inventories or stockpiles. Alternatively, these weapons may be obtained through commercially moti-vated sales to unauthorized sellers. Sometimes, these weapons are transferred to politically motivated non-state actors with the knowledge and approval of the government through the grey market.[12]

In many armed conflicts small arms and light weapons kill more people than heavy weapons. Most of Southeast Asia's ethnic conflicts and domestic insurgencies are involved in the illegal small arms trade. According to a study on the issue, five factors drive small arms smuggling in the region: (1) parties in intra-state conflicts need illegal sources of weapons; (2) these weapons are readily available in the region; (3) the region's land, maritime, and air boundaries are very porous and difficult to monitor and police; (4) there are many weak states in the region with limited capacity to patrol their borders, and where corruption in customs and immigration procedures is rampant; and (5) historical animosities among the countries in the region inhibit co-operation in controlling and combating arms smuggling and other transnational crimes.[13] These factors demonstrate that regional co-operation is an indispensable part of an effective regional response to this NTS challenge.

Piracy

Although piracy has been around since the first ships were built, this security threat in the Asia-Pacific region has increased dramatically in recent times. According to a recently published primer on piracy, "Terrorist ties and political agendas are the latest trend in motivation for stealing cargo and ships" and in some instances, "organized crime is behind the marauders that prey on shipping around Asian countries".[14] The Strait of Malacca between Malaysia and Indonesia is the most pirate-infested channel in the world and more than two-thirds of the attacks reported to the International Maritime Bureau (IMB) are in Asian waters. While reported incidents have tripled since the early 1990s, the first six months of 2003 bore witness to the worst six-month period in piracy monitoring. Within that period there were 234 pirate attacks, 16 deaths, and 52 people injured.

Moreover, the world's most dangerous places for maritime navigation are Indonesia's narrow sea channels and island hideouts, accounting for a quarter of all piratical incidents. As a consequence, Malaysia has considered providing armed police escorts for its vessels, and Japan, whose oil supplies pass through the Strait of Malacca, has offered joint police operations. Although Indonesia, Malaysia, and Singapore have increased their anti-piracy co-operation, their efforts fall short of the desired goal. Furthermore, concern over Japan's rise to the status of a "normal" power, that is, with military capability, has prevented its Southeast Asian neighbours from responding to Tokyo's proposals for regional co-operation in combating piracy. However, given Japan's increasing role in international peacekeeping in places such as Iraq, this Southeast Asian reticence could change.

In the light of Southeast Asia's many islands and inlets, experts fear that the region is speedily becoming a "breeding ground for pirates and terrorists".[15] This is more so given growing Muslim anger over U.S. military action in Afghanistan and Iraq. Extremist Muslims might be looking for ways to punish the United States and its allies by striking where it can generate the most terror by using vessels as floating bombs. These extremists are especially active in the South China Sea, along the shores of the Malacca Strait, and in the southern Philippines. Most of the recruits to terrorism are from places of poverty and political instability, such as Indonesia and the Philippines. Moreover, alleged ties between Al-Qaeda and Jemaah Islamiyah (JI), as well as with local terrorist groups such as the Abu Sayyaf in the Philippines, render the region vulnerable to terrorist attacks. Should piracy and terrorism combine forces, the security threat to the region could be overwhelming.

South Korea shares the region's interest in keeping the straits open and free for international navigation. Like major maritime countries, its commercial ships use the Strait of Malacca and the South China Sea to transport its goods. South Korea's military alliance with the United States is another reason for Seoul's interest in keeping the region's sea lanes of communications (SLOCs) free from piratical attacks. The U.S. Seventh fleet, which is part of the United States' security umbrella in the region, uses these waters. If the region's SLOCs are kept from pirate attacks, the ASEAN countries and South Korea would greatly benefit from renewed trade. Thus, the interests of the states in the region converge on this issue as well.

Pirates and terrorists are not the only sources of ocean-related security challenges. Security challenges are also posed by environmental degradation due to overfishing and the use of environmentally hostile fishing technologies, as well as dumping of various forms of hazardous wastes in the oceans. There are various forms of illicit activities that use the oceans for their operations. Among them are illegal drug trafficking, illegal trafficking of human beings, particularly women and children, and the proliferation of WMD.[16]

Global Terrorism

Southeast Asia has sometimes been labelled global terrorism's second front.[17] The reasons for this epithet are: (1) it is home to Indonesia, the world's largest Muslim country; (2) while other Southeast Asian countries, such as Malaysia and Brunei, have a large Muslim majority, or substantive Muslim minorities like the Philippines, Singapore, and Thailand, the region's ethnic-based secessionist movements are located in Indonesia, the Philippines, and Thailand; (3) the region's porous borders encourage infiltration by insidious forces; and (4) poverty facilitates terrorist recruitment among the population. Although Islam in Southeast Asia is moderate and modernist, extremist forces within the region's Muslim population are suspected to have joined the global terrorist networks of Al-Qaeda and JI. JI members have been reported to be training in camps controlled by the Moro Islamic Liberation Front (MILF) in the Philippines. The Balik Islam (Return to Islam) movement among Filipino converts to Islam has also been identified as a source of terrorist threat by the Philippine military and police.[18] Indonesia's reticence in acknowledging the terrorist threat within its borders was shattered by the Bali bombing incident of October 2002, the JW Marriot Hotel bombing in Jakarta in 2003, and the second Bali bombings in October 2005. The confessions of a number of Muslim extremists arrested in Malaysia in December 2001, the Philippines in January 2001, Singapore in December 2001 and May 2002, and Thailand in August 2003 have confirmed the authorities' belief in the existence of a regional terrorist network[19] and the notion that Southeast Asia is a second front in the war against terrorism.

The Philippines joined the coalition against terrorism (and by extension, the war in Iraq). Singapore and Thailand also support the campaign. Indonesia and Malaysia were neither keen on the idea nor critical of the United States' approach to international terrorism. Some of the ASEAN states forged a number of multilateral and bilateral agreements to combat terrorism. Some of these agreements are limited to ASEAN states while other agreements are with outside partners such as the United States, Australia, China, India, and Russia.[20] ASEAN countries already have ongoing exchange programmes involving information and intelligence, as well as military personnel and law enforcement agents. They also conduct joint military exercises among themselves and with extra-regional powers like the United States and Australia. However, the new co-operation agreements following the 11 September attacks seek to do more in this area, including countering terrorist activities funded by money laundering. Moreover, in the aftermath of 11 September and the resultant change in the United States' security policy and its emphasis on pre-emptive strike, two Southeast Asian countries — the Philippines and Thailand — emerged as major non-North Atlantic Treaty Organization (NATO) allies of the United States. This tag provides these two countries with priority access to U.S. military assistance.

The differing positions of Southeast Asian countries on the campaign against terrorism have created some dissonance within ASEAN. Far from creating any cracks within the grouping, the ASEAN states collectively signed an anti-terrorism co-operation pact with their dialogue partners in July 2005 in Vientiane.

Pandemic Diseases: SARS, HIV/AIDS, Avian Flu

Pandemic diseases constitute another NTS challenge affecting East Asia and other areas. The region's security environment was shaken by the eruption of the SARS pandemic in 2003. It spread quickly from southern China to Hong Kong, Singapore, Vietnam, and Canada. SARS worked in tandem with the terrorist scare to severely affect the region's tourism industry, which is a major source of foreign exchange earnings of countries like China, Indonesia, Malaysia, and Thailand. Due to its economic implications, the leaders of ASEAN and China joined forces and put up a US$1.55 million fund to fight SARS. While the total economic cost of SARS may not be readily determined just yet, it is certain that Taiwanese exports to Hong Kong in May 2003 fell by 30 per cent. Similarly, Taiwanese investments in China, concentrated in Jiangsu (40 per cent), Guangdong (32 per cent), and Fujian (8.7 per cent), declined in January-April 2003 from an increase of 74 per cent in 2002 to an increase of only 22 per cent in April 2003; during the same period, new contracts signed fell by 73 per cent.[21]

While the disease has abated, it is expected to recur (as it had) with the onset of winter. Cases of SARS were reported in Singapore, Taiwan, and southern China in late 2003, and again in 2004. While the Singapore and Taiwan cases were of workers in research laboratories studying the disease, the Chinese case occurred near the capital of Guangdong Province where SARS originated. The SARS outbreak revealed flaws in China's system of governance and the extent to which its leadership would keep the outside world from knowing about the dangerous disease for reasons of national interest but from which its international image also suffered.[22] Like terrorism, SARS is used to put national security as a government priority, thereby impairing the observance of civil liberties, the rule of law, and due process in some countries.

On the other hand, the spread of HIV/AIDS in the region has been widely recognized. The disease came into prominence through the region's sex tourism industry, overseas contract workers, and seafarers. Its spread is compounded by inadequate information and health care as well as poor monitoring. As a result, the spread of the disease has reached serious proportions, particularly in three ASEAN countries in recent years. According to the United Nations Programme on HIV/AIDS (UNAIDS), this epidemic shows no signs of abating, with rapid increases in newer epidemics in Asia (and Eastern Europe). Five million people were infected with HIV worldwide and 3 million died in 2003.[23] Three ASEAN countries have already had to contend with the disease — Cambodia, Myanmar, and Thailand — while Vietnam faces the possibility of a serious epidemic, where injecting drug users constitute 65 per cent of those infected by the disease.[24]

In 2004 and 2005 Asia had to contend with the spread of avian flu from China to Vietnam, Thailand, and Indonesia. Avian flu caused another threat to the physical and economic security of people, particularly those who are in the poultry business. Millions of chickens were slaughtered across the affected countries in an effort to stem the spread of the disease. Avian flu has since spread to other parts of East Asia (including Japan) and beyond (such as Turkey). In the meantime, the lessons of the SARS epidemic appear to have been lost on leaders of some countries, for there was a general lack of immediate and full disclosure of the eruption of the disease. As an upshot, this inefficient handling of the outbreak could be responsible for its wide contagion effect.

Energy Crisis

Rapid economic development in East Asia has contributed greatly to the region's increasing demand for energy supplies. Indonesia, which had hitherto been a net oil exporter, has now become a net importer. China, which had hitherto exported crude oil to its "friends", has become one of the world's largest oil consumers and importers. India's global search for energy has altered some of its major foreign and security policy thrusts as well.

According to the Institute for the Analysis of Global Security (IAGS), since the world's shift from coal to oil as a major energy source, countries the world over have consumed over 875 billion barrels of oil. It is predicted that from now till 2020, world oil consumption will rise by 60 per cent. By 2025 the number of vehicles will increase to 1.25 billion from the present 700 million; this could in turn lead to a doubling of the world's petrol consumption. India and China account for a third of humanity's highest growth in oil consumption.[25]

Many of the world's leading oil-producing countries are politically unstable and/or have difficult relations with the United States. Two-thirds of the world's oil reserves are located in the Middle East, a volatile region where the United States is most disliked. At the other end of the spectrum, the record of the Organization of Petroleum Exporting Countries (OPEC) in human rights, political stability, and compliance with international law leaves much to be desired – 22 per cent of the world's oil is in the hands of state-sponsored terrorism and under United Nations or U.S. sanctions; only 9 per cent is in the hands of countries considered free by Freedom House.

The energy crisis is also linked to international terrorism. Terrorist organizations have great interest in targeting oil and gas facilities. Al-Qaeda has identified the world's energy system as a soft underbelly whose destruction is certain to deliver a major blow to global economic security. Hence, the Al-Qaeda attacks in Riyadh, Osama bin Laden's emissaries seeking to unite Islamic groups in Nigeria under Al-Qaeda, threats from Islamic groups in Central Asia, and JI's activities in Southeast Asia, particularly in Indonesia and the Philippines.

The world's oil routes are used by some 3,500 tankers, which are marked by choke points. As a result, they are highly vulnerable to attacks. As these choke points are in straight and narrow channels, they can be easily blocked by pirates and terrorists. Thirty per cent of the world's trade and 80 per cent of Japan's crude oil pass through the Strait of Malacca. Thus, the energy crisis is an important NTS challenge as it is linked to other NTS issues. ASEAN states (with the possible exception of Brunei, Malaysia, and Myanmar) as well as South Korea share the need for energy imports. Thus, piracy and international terrorism could be areas of enhanced security co-operation between them.

Natural Disasters and Environmental Degradation

Natural disasters and environmental degradation constitute a security challenge that has only come to the fore of public scrutiny in recent years. This is not necessarily because they are related to violence, but because they threaten human security. They are not often regarded as a security challenge because natural disasters are sporadic events taking place on short notice. However, it has to be acknowledged that their aftermath could be hugely devastating to lives and properties, as shown by the *tsunami* disaster of December 2004 and hurricane Katrina in late August 2005. Environmental degradation takes a while to manifest itself. As it is a "slow boil" issue, most people tend to regard environmental degradation as a matter of low priority. Even in places recently hit by environmental degradation, such as the flash flooding in Quezon Province, Philippines, in 2004, the loss of lives and properties did little to promote awareness about the need to protect communities from the destructive effects of environmental degradation. The irreparable loss of lives and land wrought by environmental degradation shows that it is a major challenge. After the usual knee-jerk response through a total log ban, sector interests have once again reverted to importuning the government to return to a business-as-usual approach.

Both South Korea and ASEAN countries are affected by natural disasters and environmental degradation. Southeast Asia is vulnerable to typhoons, earthquakes, and *tsunami*, situated as it is in the world's typhoon belt and its "ring of fire". Haze from forest fires in Indonesia has periodically affected its neighbours, particularly Singapore, Malaysia, Thailand, and the Philippines, to the extent that the grouping has agreed to forge closer co-operation in this NTS area.

On the other hand, South Korea's main environmental challenge comes from the effects of its own and China's rapid industrialization as well as from climate change bringing drought to its neighbour to the north. The latter constitutes another form of security challenge to the region as North Koreans affected by prolonged droughts have moved across borders in search of food. Moreover, environmental destruction has resulted in many North Koreans fleeing to South Korea through China. In turn, food aid from South Korea and the United States is linked to Pyongyang's nuclear weapons development programme, which is another regional security challenge.[26]

VARYING SECURITY PERSPECTIVES: ASEAN AND SOUTH KOREA

It is noteworthy that South Korea has not been mentioned as often as other East Asian countries in the above discussion of NTS issues facing the region. South Korea's absence in these various NTS issues is due to its different perspectives on security issues. Unlike Japan and China, which meet traditional security threats head on with comprehensive and co-operative security, South Korea appears wedded to the traditional realist perspective of security. This could be a function both of its history — past and present — as well as its geostrategic and geopolitical profile.

As a divided nation, Koreans tend to put a higher premium on traditional security concerns *vis-à-vis* Southeast Asians. North and South Korean troops have been locked to do ready battle across the demilitarized zone (DMZ) for decades. The unabated nuclear weapons development programme of Pyongyang continues to pose a serious security challenge to Seoul and its neighbours. Thus, while its Southeast Asian neighbours are preoccupied by varying levels of low-intensity conflict at the domestic front, South Korea has been facing serious military security threats from Pyongyang since the 1950s. It did not help that Beijing and Moscow traditionally supported Pyongyang until the 1990s. While the six-party talks could ameliorate tension on the Korean Peninsula, their contribution to a real reduction and eventual elimination of North Korea's military threat to South Korea remains inconclusive.

South Korea's location between two major powers whose eventual relationship remains fluid (that is, as both strategic partners and strategic competitors) also contributes to the nation's sense of unease. There remain key unresolved issues between China and Japan, including territorial and historical. The unfolding of these issues is likely to affect South Korea. Cross-strait relations have also been highly unstable during the past decade, largely fuelled by volatile political developments in Taiwan and the emergence of new nationalism in China in tandem with its impressive and sustained economic surge. China's maintenance that Taiwan is a renegade province is backed by its unequivocal commitment to use force should Taiwan move towards independence. This is a development that is likely to drag the United States into the fray. As it is situated in the midst of these tensions, South Korea is not immune to these strategic developments.

ASEAN and South Korea also differ in the extent to which they are affected by NTS issues. As seen in the previous discussion of these issues facing the region, ASEAN countries appear to be more directly affected by all of them — from illegal trafficking in drugs, human beings, and small arms and light weapons to piracy, global terrorism, and pandemic diseases. Various CSCAP studies on NTS issues, including transnational crime, point to this reality, such as the trafficking in illegal drugs, human beings, and small arms and light weapons. South Koreans recognize this as a problem but feel it is not a high priority in their country.[27] As already noted, they feel more threatened by environmental pollution, particularly manifested in acid rain originating from China.[28]

IMPERATIVES FOR STRENGTHENING CO-OPERATION IN NON-TRADITIONAL SECURITY ISSUES

Nevertheless, there are a number of important imperatives for strengthening bilateral co-operation in NTS issues. Among them are:

Firstly, the transborder character of the NTS challenges facing the region. Particularly relevant are measures for combating piracy, global terrorism, pandemic diseases, as well as adopting protection measures in the face of the energy crisis, natural disasters, and environmental degradation. Piracy and terrorism are the most fearsome as they have the ability to further compound the effects of global terrorism by impinging on the security of people and states. This is particularly so if pirates and terrorists use ships as explosive devices to attack megaports in Singapore, South Korea, Japan, or elsewhere in the region. They are also linked to energy security. All these have direct implications for South Korea and ASEAN; and as such, should be areas for strengthening their bilateral relationship through enhancing security co-operation.

Secondly, their common vision for an East Asia community provides another impetus for enhanced co-operation. If the ASEAN vision for "a community of caring societies" is to be realized, the reduction, if not complete elimination, of social ills covering all the NTS issues discussed herein would be an integral component of such caring societies. Such recognition is evident in many of the EASG Report's twenty-two key recommendations and its seventeen concrete short-term measures and nine concrete medium- and long-term measures. Especially important is the EASG's short-term measure to "strengthen mechanisms for cooperation on non-traditional security issues" and medium- and long-term measures to "promote closer regional marine environmental cooperation for the entire region, [and] build a framework for energy policies and strategies and action plans".

Thirdly, South Korea and ASEAN have a common responsibility to make this side of the ASEAN plus Three triangle of bilateral relationship develop in tandem with the other two bilateral relationships.

CONCLUDING REMARKS

Given the numerous realities and recent developments, there are ample reasons and opportunites to strengthen ASEAN–South Korea ties through their joint co-operation in NTS issues. The common NTS challenges they face provide the impetus for their mutual co-operation in this area. Recent improvements, such as the inclusion of political and security issues in their dialogues and the signing of a co-operation pact to combat terrorism, are hopeful signs that have to be further encouraged. Indeed, the establishment of an East Asia community based on the ASEAN plus Three process requires no less.

NOTES

1. During the First East Asia Summit held in Kuala Lumpur in December 2005, ASEAN and South Korea agreed to complete the negotiations for this purpose.

2. This section is drawn from the author's following papers: "Transnational Security Issues: Implications for the Region" (Philippine Army Senior Leaders Conference, Armed Forces of the Philippines, Fort Bonifacio, 18 March 2004); and "The Security Environment in ASEAN Since 9/11: An ASEAN Perspective" (Paper prepared for an international conference on Reassessing Japan–ASEAN Relations: Between Expectations and Realities, ISEAS, Singapore, 30 September–1 October 2003). See also Carolina G. Hernandez and Gina R. Pattugalan, eds., *Transnational Crime and Regional Security in the Asia Pacific* (Quezon City: Institute for Strategic and Development Studies, Inc. and Council for Security Cooperation in the Asia Pacific, 1999) on transnational crime as a security threat to the region.

3. "Illegal Drug Trafficking Represents 8% of World Trade, Says UN Report", August 1997, http://www.ndsn.org/AUGUST97/UNREPORT.html.

4. Pierre-Arnaud Chouvy, "New drug trafficking routes in Southeast Asia", *Jane's Intelligence Review*, 1 July 2003, http://www.pa-chouvy.org/JIR2.htm, posted on 19 June 2002.

5. U.S. Department of State, "Trafficking in Persons Report", released by the Office to Monitor and Combat Trafficking in Persons on 11 June 2003, http://sss.state.gov/g/tip/rls/tiprpt/2003/21262.htm, accessed on 6 January 2004.

6. U.S. Department of State, "Trafficking in Persons Report, June 2005", http://state.gov/g/tip/rls/tiprpt/2005, accessed on 10 January 2006.

7. UNIFEM Gender Fact Sheet, no. 2, "Trafficking in Women and Children", undated.

8. Global March Against Child Labor, "Child Trafficking Statistics around the World", http://www.globalmarch.org/child-trafficking/statistics.html, 74 pages, accessed on 31 December 2003.

9. The Study Group is scheduled to submit its report to the CSCAP Steering Committee in December 2006.

10. David Capie, "Sovereignty Under Fire: Small Arms Smuggling in Southeast Asia", *Panorama* 3, no. 1 (Manila: Konrad Adenauer Stiftung, 2001), p. 58.

11. Ibid., pp. 61–62.

12. Ibid., p. 62.

13. David Capie, "Small arms production and transfer in Southeast Asia", *Canberra Papers on Strategy and Defence*, no. 146 (Canberra: Australian National University, 2002), p. 15.

14. Virtual Information Center, *Primer: Piracy in Asia*, Honolulu, USCINCPAC, updated on 31 October 2003, www.secure-marine.com/piracy_update.pdf, p. 2.

15. Ibid., p. 24.

16. Carolina G. Hernandez, "Regional Cooperation in Maritime Security" (Paper presented at the Maritime Symposium on The Philippines as a Maritime State: Setting the Foundations for Strategizing National Development and Security,

Philippine Navy, Armed Forces of the Philippines Commissioned Officers' Country Club, Camp General Emilio Aguinaldo, Quezon City, 16–17 May 2005).

17. Woodrow Wilson International Center for Scholars, Asia Program Special Report, *Fighting Terrorism on the Southeast Asian Front* (Washington, D.C., June 2003).

18. Among the Balik Islam groups is the Rajah Sulaiman Group, which claimed responsibility for the bombing of the Super Ferry in Manila in 2005.

19. Carolina G. Hernandez, "Terrorist Networks in Southeast Asia: Implications for Regional Security" (Paper prepared for the Seventh Asia-Pacific Security Forum, Global Governance in the Light of New Security Developments, INPR, Pacific Forum/CSIS, IFRI, and ISDS, Taipei, 30 November–1 December 2003).

20. A list of these agreements can be found in Carolina G. Hernandez, "Fighting Terrorism in Southeast Asia: A View from the Philippines", in *Fighting Terrorism on the Southeast Asian Front*, pp. 25–30.

21. Christopher R. Hughes, "SARS as a Non-Traditional Security Threat" (Paper presented to the Asia-Pacific Security Forum, Taipei, 29 November–1 December 2003).

22. See Hughes, op. cit., for a comprehensive discussion of this issue.

23. UNAIDS Press Release, London, 25 November 2003.

24. UNAIDS, "Asia and the Pacific", Fact sheet, December 2003.

25. This section is culled from a study on oil by the Institute for the Analysis of Global Security, 2005.

26. Shin-wha Lee, "Safeguarding the Environment: An Agenda for Regional Cooperation in South Korea, Northeast Asia, and Beyond", in *Population, Food, Energy, and the Environment: Challenges to Asia–Europe Cooperation*, edited by Carolina G. Hernandez and Gill Wilkins (Quezon City: Institute for Strategic and Development Studies and Council for Asia–Europe Cooperation, 2000), pp. 182–212.

27. See Hernandez and Pattugalan, op. cit.

28. Lee, op. cit.

5

How to Counter "New" Terrorism

Kang Choi

SEARCH FOR NEW SECURITY PARADIGM IN THE POST-COLD WAR ERA

One of the most distinctive characteristics of the post-Cold War era is the substantial reduction of inter-state conflicts involving massive use of physical force. On the other hand, the so-called non-conventional security threats, such as terrorism, proliferation of weapons of mass destruction (WMD), religious and ethnic conflicts, environmental degradation, drug trafficking, piracy, and organized crimes, have become more immediate security concerns. Such a transition has expanded the scope of security well beyond simple military security. In other words, we are living in an era of comprehensive security. Before these new security challenges can be met effectively and successfully, the establishment of a new security paradigm and approaches is necessary.

Such new security challenges are not confined, or limited, geographically to a specific region or country. Rather they are challenges to humanity as a whole, or transnational security challenges. These challenges cannot be handled by any single nation alone, as traditional alliance structures are too rigid, slow, and reactive to cope with new security challenges.

On the other hand, military responses in countering new security challenges over the past several years since the 11 September incident have been dominant. Furthermore, due to the progress made in science and technology, especially information, communication, and computers, the level and magnitude of damage from the actual use of force have substantially decreased. As such, the possibility of actual use of force, including frequency and form,[1] is rather likely to increase. It implies that more physical means are nowadays available for the attainment of political and military objectives. Thus, we are more tempted to use force before exhausting other means.

In sum, with the changes in the security environment and the emergence of new security challenges, a new security paradigm reflecting the nature and magnitude of the current and upcoming security challenges is needed. Among these new security challenges, terrorism requires immediate intellectual attention and strategic response.

CHARACTERISTICS AND EFFECTS OF "NEW" TERRORISM

It can be said that traditional terrorism, such as assassination and kidnapping of VIPs, hijacking of airplanes, and hostage taking, is rather limited in nature and directed towards certain specific targets. But new terrorism is quite different from traditional terrorism.

The 11 September attacks were an unprecedented form of terrorism, equivalent to the level of a small-scale war. Despite our efforts to strengthen international control regimes on WMD, more nuclear material has become available. There is a growing concern that the possible connection of terrorism and WMD might cause a catastrophe tantamount to another world war.

Dramatic economic and social progress renders nations unable to have full control, and vulnerable to crippling and unexpected terrorist attacks. The vulnerability stems from the growing complexity and interconnectedness of our modern societies. In particular, progress in information processing and dependence on the Internet only amplify the destructive power of terrorists, thus worsening the current situation.

Simultaneously, growing technological capacity and information have resulted in more diverse and abundant opportunities to divert state-of-the-art technologies to counter the terrorists' destructive weapons. It should be noted that the 11 September attacks were a complex form of terrorism involving the combination of hijacking and suicide bombing. This new kind of mass violence uses a high-energy vehicle (the airplane) to carry out terrorism. Progress in precision, portability, and miniaturization of weapons has brought ease-of-use and affordability to destructive means of power. Today, such technological changes make it easier to cause mass casualties and chaos at a low cost. In addition, new information technology allows terrorists and other malicious individuals to magnify their own disruptive power by sharing information on weapons and tactics globally.

All nations have become wide-open targets for terrorists, who spread fear throughout the international community. Today's terrorist attacks, unlike those in the past when a particular person was targeted, aim at indiscriminately creating mass casualties, as seen in Bali, Madrid, and London. No one is free from the threat of terrorism. As can be witnessed in the attacks, the goal of terrorism is not only to inflict physical damage but also to create widespread panic and social chaos.

It is possible to notice a shift in terrorism motives and the growing conflicts that follow. Terrorist groups based on ideological or political agenda in the past are now driven by religious and ethnic hatred, or by cultural mis-understanding. Increasingly, terrorism and counter-terrorism activities have created cultural and religious conflicts among nation states. Furthermore, the changing perception of terrorism makes it harder to prepare follow-up measures to counter future terrorism.

Terrorism in the past was less difficult to trace and penetrate. However, new terrorist groups rely on affiliations with like-minded amateurs with religious beliefs and social frustration. Such people pursue their terrorist campaign at the cost of their own lives. Unlike experts who minded their own survival, it is difficult to predict the likelihood of today's terrorist attack in advance.

CURRENT STATUS OF COUNTER-TERRORISM ACTIVITIES

There are twelve conventions and protocols in combating terrorism.[2] All the international treaties and protocols that came into effect were designed to defend against a particular form of terrorism; as a result, their scope to prevent and take countermeasures against today's complex form of terrorism is limited. Due to the lack of comprehensiveness and generality in response, such institutional tools cannot effectively deter and defend against new forms of terrorism. The United Nations (UN) and other regional security organizations have made continuous efforts to counter terrorism. The UN Security Council adopted Resolution 1373, which established the Counter-Terrorism Committee (CTC) and imposed binding obligations on all 191 UN member states. It calls upon all states to report to the CTC on the steps taken to implement Resolution 1373. The CTC, with the assistance of ten experts, then reviews reports and drafts a letter to the relevant states asking a series of follow-up questions to be answered in the state's subsequent report.

Historically, the North Atlantic Treaty Organization (NATO) and European countries have long experienced small-scale "old terrorism", which is substantially different from that suddenly faced by the United States. Naturally, this means that they have been taking different approaches to fighting terrorism. There are divergences in the concept of security, capacity, and political priorities between the European Union (EU) and the United States. Most European authorities have pursued follow-up measures rather than the prevention of terrorism. As an open border is integral to the expansion of the EU, there is less haste among European authorities to tighten border control and improve homeland security. After the 11 September attacks, European countries showed greater concern about the possibility of large-scale mass-casualty attacks and have introduced measures to initiate joint investigations of endemic criminal problems and provide co-operation with other European countries. Positive steps, such as intelligence exchanges between the EU and the United States and airport patrol, are being pursued. However, it is unlikely that the EU will take homeland security measures similar to those of the United States.

Despite the apparent difference in capability and domestic constraints to counter terrorism, ASEAN countries have demonstrated efforts for increased co-operation and exchange of information among the interior ministries and intelligence services since the 11 September attacks. While there is growing discontent and suspicion over the highly militarized approach of the U.S. counter-terrorism strategy throughout the region, the ASEAN Ministerial Meeting on Transnational Crime (AMMTC) has been the engine of enhanced co-operation among ASEAN countries to create substantial levels of counter-terrorism collaboration between and among the ASEAN states and their partner countries. As ASEAN countries are fully aware that terrorism is not merely a danger to innocents but a threat to economic prosperity as well, there is a growing consensus on the exchange of ideas and information about the best practices for combating terrorism.

The United States–ASEAN Joint Declaration on Combating Terrorism of August 2002 is an example of the commitment of both sides to closer intelligence exchange and co-operation. Another example of the concerted co-operation is the signing of the Anti-Terrorism Pact by Malaysia, Indonesia, and the Philippines in May 2002. ASEAN countries have made collective expressions through declarations and reaffirm a shared political commitment to combating the regional terrorist threat. Encountering several domestic restrictions, however, the ASEAN authorities have been slow in taking decisive action due to: weak immigration control and porous borders; longstanding trade and economic links with Middle East countries; widespread criminal activities; smuggling of small-sized weapons; lack of professionalism, training, and competence of intelligence and security agencies; broad bureaucratic rivalries among agencies; conflict between authoritative regimes and Islamic groups; and lack of capacity to monitor vast and remote areas.

The United States co-operates with the ASEAN countries to avoid the formation of the second front in the Asian region. As the ASEAN countries worry about America's military-centric unilateral and coercive strategy, which is often viewed as religious and cultural conflicts among nation states, Asia's current problems are unlikely to be resolved without addressing the root causes of terrorism. Accordingly, considerations not only in the socio-economic dimension but also within the ideological and religious dimension of terrorism are required.

Since the 11 September attacks counter-terrorism efforts and responses have changed from a reactive to a proactive and preventive mode in a more comprehensive way. It engages in multidimensional and multifaceted approaches. Along this line bilateral, sub-regional, regional, and international efforts are simultaneously sought in a mutually reinforcing and complementary manner. There is a strong universal consensus on the need to eradicate terrorism and, furthermore, grounds for counter-terrorism are expected to be more solid and universal. Notably, information and intelligence exchanges have been strengthened. Likewise, stricter measures for border control and the movement of people have been introduced in most countries.

Despite all such whole-hearted efforts and the universal consensus in principle to counter terrorism, there are many things still to be resolved, from the definition of terrorism to legal and jurisdictional issues.

First, in order to have a comprehensive convention on countering terrorism, it is necessary to have a common definition of terrorism. But, due to the absence of a commonly agreed upon and accepted definition of terrorism, it is very difficult to introduce a comprehensive treaty or convention on counter-terrorism. The same person, or a group, can be regarded differently, either as a terrorist or freedom fighter, depending on one's point of view.

Second, too much emphasis is put on military measures in countering terrorism. Such emphasis has tended to breed differences and has resulted in a widening gap among the concerned countries seeking to meet the challenges of terrorism. In turn, given the cultural and religious differences and orientation, it may foster a so-called "clash of civilizations".

Third, closely related to the above fact, unilateralism in countering terrorism is one of the most controversial issues. Nowadays we often observe the exercise of unilateralism in countering terrorism. In order to consolidate the background for counter-terrorism efforts, it is desirable and necessary to have consensus not only in principle but also in selecting means. But such efforts have rather been neglected. In the name of counter-terrorism, human rights can be violated. Thus, ways to reconcile the conflicting natures of counter-terrorism and human rights must be sought.

Fourth, despite the desirability of a universal standard and application, it is not easy to apply a universal enforcement measure in countering terrorism, given each state's legal and political constraints. Each political entity has its own distinctive political, social, historic, and cultural background and factors. While it is desirable to have common forms and practices in meeting the challenges of terrorism, in reality, the parties concerned are constrained by differences in political, social, economic, and cultural areas.

Fifth, many things can be done to strengthen the status and functions of the CTC. Nowadays, the CTC is primarily focusing on reviewing the reports submitted by the states. However, there could be discrepancies between the text and the practice. Thus, as a checking mechanism, a field survey function must be added to uncover more about the reality. The CTC has only ten personnel, which is too small a number to carry out the missions mandated and authorized by Resolution 1373. Financial resources are much needed to ensure the effective management and operations of the CTC. If we would like to see the CTC functioning like the OPCW and IAEA, more personnel and financial resources are required; further institutionalization is also necessary.

WAYS TO ENHANCE INTERNATIONAL CO-OPERATION IN COUNTERING TERRORISM

First, we need to have a universally acceptable common definition of terrorism as a background for introducing a comprehensive counter-terrorism regime. At this stage, it is difficult to suggest a concrete definition. But, if we approach this problem from a human security perspective, it would be possible to overcome the dispute between human rights and counter-terrorism and the controversy over unilateralism.

Second, based upon human security concepts and the definition of terror, it would be desirable to have a comprehensive counter-terrorism convention. With the increased diversification of terrorist forms, the existing terrorism-related conventions or agreements appear to be limited and outdated. We must introduce a comprehensive counter-terrorism convention and related protocols based on the principle of generality and universality.

Third, to ensure implementation and compliance, it is necessary to have an executive agency like the IAEA and OPCW, similar to that of the NPT and CWC under the Sixth Committee of the UN and UN Security Council.

Without an executive agency, compliance and implementation cannot be assured. Therefore an executive agency must be formed to perform the following functions: information/intelligence gathering/integration/analysis/ production/dissemination, education and training, and co-ordination and oversight over policies on terrorism. It is possible to convert the current CTC into a more authoritative body in countering terrorism by adding functions such as education, training, information/data bank, and standby arrangements as we have in the case of the peace-keeping operation (PKO).

Fourth, regional-level efforts must be sought along with international efforts in a mutually reinforcing and complementary way. Regional organizations, such as the EU, NATO, and ASEAN, and sub-regional organizations must pay closer attention to new kinds of terrorism and must be the venue for consulting and seeking ways to meet the challenges of the new terrorism. For example, they could strengthen regional measures such as controlling and monitoring movements of people and small-arms sales. Furthermore, by taking into account regional characteristics, these regional organizations could come up with measures that are more acceptable to the parties involved.

Fifth, at the national level each state must introduce more effective counter-terrorism organizational infrastructure and legal standards. Inter-agency co-ordination sometimes appears to be quite difficult due to organizational interests of the agencies involved. Thus, central co-ordination and oversight function must be introduced to ensure the effectiveness of counter-terrorism efforts among law-enforcement agencies, intelligence agencies, and the military. Based on universality and generality, related laws and directives must be reviewed and amended, if necessary.

Sixth, the authority of the International Criminal Court must be strengthened with regard to the issue of terrorism. This would reduce, if not eliminate, the controversy over jurisdictions and terrorism. It would also contribute to the universal application of a legal standard regarding terrorism, and, in consequence, it would help us avoid projection and imposition of individual standards towards other related parties.

Last, but not least, we must seek ways to deal with the sources and rationale of terrorism, that is, terrorism's political, social, economic, and cultural reasons. While it may take time to get these problems and issues solved, it is necessary if we really intend to eradicate terrorism globally. Promotion of political dialogue for the peaceful resolution of the issue must be sought. For example, the Middle East peace process must be pursued thoroughly and whole-heartedly under the principle of peaceful co-existence. The role of the UN must be strengthened as the honest broker and mediator. Religious and cultural backgrounds of terrorism must be handled with respect for cultural diversity and humanity. The spirit of mutual respect and recognition must be observed. Regional organizations must become more active in preventing conflict from arising. The promotion of dialogue among the parties concerned is very crucial. Regional security dialogue (if any) must be strengthened.

To meet the challenges of social and economic sources of terrorism, the contributions of advanced countries are imperative. The Official Development Aid (ODA) must be reviewed from the perspective of humanity, rather than from a political angle. Financial assistance and issue-oriented assistance or project-based assistance are expected to reduce social and economic grounds for terrorism. While doing so, we should take care to avoid the imposition of our own values and ideas upon others. Our approach must be based on cultural and political diversity. Much effort must go into mobilizing and securing the international community's consensus so that the challenges of terrorism may be met.

NOTES

1. The Nuclear Posture Review (NPR), in which the United States is seeking to have more nuclear options available, can be viewed as an indicator of such a trend.
2. These are: Convention on Offences and Certain Other Acts Committed on Board Aircraft; Convention for the Unlawful Seizure of Aircraft; Convention for the Suppression of Unlawful Acts against the Safety of Civil Aviation; Convention for the Prevention and Punishment of Crimes Against Internationally Protected Persons; Protocol for the Suppression of Unlawful Acts of Violence at Airports Serving International Civil Aviation; International Convention against the Taking of Hostages; Convention on Physical Protection of Nuclear Material; International Convention for the Suppression of Terrorist Bombing; Convention on the Making of Plastic Explosives for the Purpose of Detection; Convention for the Suppression of Unlawful Acts against the Safety of Maritime Navigation; Protocol for the Suppression of Unlawful Acts against the Safety of Fixed Platforms Located on the Continental Shelf; and International Convention for the Suppression of Terrorist Financing.

REFERENCES

Martin, John R., ed. *Defeating Terrorism: Strategic Issue Analyses.* Carlisle Barracks, PA: Strategic Studies Institute, U.S. Army War College, 2002.

McFarlane, John. *Organised Crime and Terrorism in the Asia-Pacific Region: The Reality and the Response.* Canberra: Strategic and Defence Studies Centre, Australian National University, 2002.

Singh, Daljit. *The Post-September 11 Geostrategic Landscape and Southeast Asian Response to the Threat of Terrorism.* Singapore: Institute of Southeast Asian Studies, 2002.

PART III
Economic Co-operation
and FTA

6

ASEAN–Korea Economic Co-operation: Thailand's Perspective

Chanin Mephokee

BACKGROUND

Encouraged by the success of surging exports following its first free trade agreement (FTA) with Chile in 2004, South Korea unveiled an ambitious plan to push for FTAs with more than fifteen countries by 2007. To achieve its goal, South Korea has launched negotiations with fifty trading partners worldwide. It is believed that the FTAs would ensure more benefits for South Korea's export-driven economy. After all, South Korea is the world's eleventh largest economy. According to Trade Minister Kim Hyun-Chong, a long-term strategy to expand trade through a liberalized economy with less trade barriers is necessary for the South Korean economy, as it is presently facing unfavourable external conditions, such as soaring oil prices, the stronger won against the U.S. dollar, and more non-tariff trade barriers. Therefore, the FTA is the solution for South Korean companies to gain access in foreign markets.

However, South Korea has lagged far behind other members of the World Trade Organization (WTO) in free trade accords. Before South Korea concluded its accord with Chile in March 2004, it was one of only two WTO members not party to any FTA, the other being Mongolia. Presently, the country is in negotiations to eliminate trade barriers with sixteen nations, including the ASEAN states, Canada, the four-member European Free Trade Association (EFTA), and Japan.

Joint research is being conducted with seven nations, including India, Mexico, and Russia, on the feasibility of free trade negotiations. Moreover, South Korea has also established plans for negotiations with twenty-seven nations, such as the United States, China, and the European Union (EU).

South Korea and ASEAN have a long history of economic partnerships. They first established sectoral dialogue relations in November 1989. South Korea was accorded Full Dialogue Partner status by ASEAN at the Twenty-fourth ASEAN Ministerial Meeting (AMM) in July 1991 in Kuala Lumpur.

In order to enhance ASEAN–South Korea economic co-operation, the leaders of ASEAN and South Korea expressed their commitment towards the development of a comprehensive partnership at the ASEAN–South Korea Summit on 8 October 2003 in Bali, Indonesia. They tasked their ministers to discuss the possibility of establishing a free trade area. Subsequently, an ASEAN–Korea Experts Group (AKEG) was established to draw up the Joint Study Report on the feasibility of an ASEAN–South Korea FTA (AKFTA). The Joint Study has since been completed. One of the key recommendations is to realize the AKFTA by 2009 (one year earlier than the completion of the ASEAN–China FTA) between ASEAN-Six and South Korea. This is with due consideration for special and differential treatment for the developing countries of ASEAN and additional flexibility for the newer ASEAN countries, namely Cambodia, Laos, Myanmar, and Vietnam (CLMV). CLMV would be given an additional five years to realize the FTA. According to the plan, 80 per cent of their products would enjoy zero tariffs by 2009, and non-tariff products would account for 96 per cent of the total on both sides by 2015.

South Korea signed an FTA with Singapore on 4 August 2005 in Seoul. It is the second South Korean FTA after its agreement with Chile. According to the agreement, the two sides would remove tariffs on most of their goods and services within ten years. As planned, South Korea would be signing an FTA with ASEAN at the ASEAN–South Korea Summit in December 2005.

ASEAN–SOUTH KOREA ECONOMIC RELATIONS

ASEAN and South Korea are important trading partners. The volume of trade between these two entities has been growing remarkably. In 2003

ASEAN became South Korea's fifth-largest trading partner, accounting for 10.4 per cent of South Korea's total trade volume. ASEAN exported to South Korea US$17.1 billion or 4 per cent of ASEAN's total exports to the world and imported from South Korea US$15.1 billion or 4.2 per cent of ASEAN's total world imports (Table 6.1).

Table 6.1
South Korean Exports to and Imports from ASEAN, 1996–2004
(US$ million)

	Total Exports	Exports to ASEAN	Percentage Share (%)	Total Imports	Imports from ASEAN	Percentage Share (%)
1996	129,715	20,311	15.7	150,339	12,074	8.0
1997	136,164	20,365	15.0	144,616	12,549	8.7
1998	132,313	15,328	11.6	93,282	9,135	9.8
1999	143,685	17,708	12.3	119,752	12,250	10.2
2000	172,268	20,134	11.7	160,481	18,173	11.3
2001	150,439	16,459	10.9	141,098	15,916	11.3
2002	162,471	18,400	11.3	152,126	16,757	11.0
2003	193,817	20,253	10.4	178,827	18,459	10.3
2004	207,591	19,800	9.5	183,058	18,220	10.0

Source: Kwon Yul, "Toward a Comprehensive Partnership: ASEAN–Korea Economic Cooperation", *East Asian Review* 16, no. 4 (2004): 81–98.

South Korean investment in ASEAN has generally accounted for about 3 per cent of the total foreign direct investment (FDI) flowing into ASEAN during 1995–2003. However, South Korea's cumulative investments in ASEAN amount to US$11 billion or 15.2 per cent of South Korea's total FDI outflow, making ASEAN the third-largest investment destination for South Korean firms.

Products that ASEAN has comparative advantages over South Korea are prepared foodstuffs, mineral products, wood, and wood products. South Korean products with comparative advantages over the ASEAN states are textiles and apparel, base metal and metal articles, machinery and electrical appliances, and automobiles.

The ASEAN states import mainly machinery and electrical appliances, base metal, and chemical products from South Korea. The main markets for South Korean machinery and electrical appliances are Singapore, Malaysia, the Philippines, and Thailand. The important markets for base metal are Malaysia, Thailand, and Singapore. The main markets for chemical products are Indonesia, Thailand, and Malaysia.

The main ASEAN products imported by South Korea are machinery and electrical appliances, mineral products, and chemical products. These products account for 80 per cent of South Korea's total imports from ASEAN. Singapore, Malaysia, and the Philippines are the main sources for machinery and electrical appliances, while Indonesia and Malaysia are the main sources for mineral products. The main sources for chemical products are Singapore, Indonesia, and Malaysia.

ASEAN and South Korea have a very long investment relationship and history. The first South Korean FDI in ASEAN was made by the South Korea Development Corporation to develop forests in Indonesia in 1968.

South Korean investment in ASEAN began to increase in the late 1980, through the 1990s. The total South Korean FDI in ASEAN was only US$16.1 million in 1985. However, the figure increased sharply to US$254.1 million by 1990 and then reached US$415.1 million in 1995. In 2003 South Korea's total investment in ASEAN reached US$508 million covering 222 projects. Liberalization of host country policies towards FDI and the comparatively lower wages in ASEAN are key inducements for South Korea's FDI.

Most of South Korea's FDI is in the manufacturing industries, such as footwear, textiles, and electronics.

Indonesia is the most significant FDI destination for South Korea, receiving 31.1 per cent. Vietnam is now an attractive destination for South Korean ventures, receiving some 22.5 per cent of their investment. However, among the ten ASEAN states, 98 per cent of South Korea's FDI is concentrated in six countries; the remaining 2 per cent goes to Myanmar, Cambodia, Laos, and Brunei (Table 6.5).

Table 6.2
South Korea's Trade Balance with ASEAN by Products, 1999–2003
(US$ million)

Items	Average Exports a Year	Average Imports a Year	Trade Balance
Prepared foodstuffs	78.7	198.1	–119.4
Mineral products	931.3	4,749.3	–3,818.0
Wood and wood articles	7.0	336.0	–330.0
Textiles and apparels	864.0	346.0	518.0
Base metal and metal articles	1,361.6	434.6	927.0
Machinery and electrical appliances	7,740.8	6,110.4	1,630.4
Automobiles	676.7	73.3	603.4
Total	14,217.4	14,589.3	–371.9

Source: <www.aseansec.org>

Table 6.3
Labour Costs per Worker in Manufacturing
(US$ per year)

Country	Labour Costs (Wages)		% Increase
	1980–84	1995–99	
Malaysia	2,519	3,429	36.1
Thailand	2,305	2,705	17.4
Indonesia	898	1,008	12.2
Philippines	1,240	2,450	97.6
Singapore	5,576	21,534	286.2
South Korea	3,153	10,743	240.7

Source: World Bank, *World Development Indicators, 2000,* pp. 58–60.

Table 6.4
South Korea's Investment in ASEAN by Sector, 2001–03
(US$ thousand)

	2001	2002	2003	Total Investment	Net Investment
Agriculture	772	592	1,247	72,018 (1.1%)	46,294 (1.1%)
Mining	11,013	23,334	114,130	584,507 (9.7%)	531,046 (13.1%)
Manufacturing	267,681	205,752	132,944	3,687,594 (61.5%)	2,404,675 (59.5%)
Construction	33,032	11,519	10,833	231,644 (3.9%)	16,208 (4.0%)
Wholesale/ Retail sale	27,774	14,789	200,581	657,416 (10.9%)	228,614 (5.7%)
Storage	954	2,573	1,594	21,744 (0.4%)	18,724 (0.5%)
Telecommunications	274	11,328	37,283	247,051 (4.1%)	229,161 (5.7%)
Finance/Insurance	5	0	0	455 (0%)	455 (0%)
Hotels/Restaurants	1,135	719	640	72,716 (6.9%)	45,513 (1.1%)
Real estate/Services	30,143	46,621	8,752	415,716 (6.9%)	378,778 (9.4%)
Others	0	54	0	54 (0%)	54 (0%)

Source: Kwon Yul, "Toward a Comprehensive Partnership: ASEAN–Korea Economic Cooperation", *East Asian Review* 16, no. 4 (2004): 81–98.

Table 6.5
South Korea's FDI Inflows to ASEAN by Country
(US$ thousand)

	2001	2002	2003	Total Remaining amount
Malaysia	19,872	6,189	6,428	334,284 (8.4%)
Thailand	30,777	31,480	26,496	528,458 (13.3%)
Indonesia	169,480	64,728	78,528	1,237,984 (31.1%)
Singapore	40,918	48,166	234,343	422,798 (10.6%)
Philippines	569,333	26,732	16,363	500,374 (12.6%)
Vietnam	46,280	135,403	136,512	880,822 (22.1%)
Cambodia	5,540	3,877	9,219	34,618 (0.9%)
Myanmar	2,948	660	0	29,678 (0.7%)
Laos	35	50	115	7,090 (0.2%)
Brunei	0	0	0	1,937 (0%)

Source: Kwon Yul, "Toward a Comprehensive Partnership: ASEAN–Korea Economic Cooperation", *East Asian Review* 16, no. 4 (2004): 81–98.

Table 6.6
South Korea's Exports to Thailand by Products
(US$ million)

	2000	2004
Electrical machinery	343.00	600.70
Machinery	150.30	370.10
Chemical products	279.70	360.70
Iron and steel	143.90	302.80
Integrated circuits	206.70	302.00

Source: Ministry of Commerce, Thailand.

Even though ASEAN as a whole is South Korea's major trading partner, Thailand is not its major trading partner. However, the volume of trade between Thailand and South Korea has been increasing continuously, so much so that South Korea enjoys a surplus in trade. The value of the trade surplus has been increasing. It reached US$1.7 billion in 2004.

The main South Korean exports to Thailand are machinery, chemical products, steel, and integrated circuits (Table 6.6). The main Thai exports to South Korea are integrated circuits, para rubber, computers and parts, radios and television sets, as well as chilled and frozen shrimps (Table 6.7).

Of the Thai products exported to South Korea 62.71 per cent are manufacturing products. Only 23.1 per cent are agricultural products. However, 58.8 per cent of South Korean exports to Thailand are raw materials and intermediate products, 31.43 per cent are capital products, and 1.99 per cent are automobiles and automobile parts.

Table 6.7
Thailand's Exports to South Korea by Products
(US$ million)

	2000	2004
Integrated circuits	173.30	260.70
Para rubber	100.90	223.90
Computers and parts	137.40	83.90
Radios and television sets	21.60	60.80
Chilled and frozen shrimps	28.30	48.10

Source: Ministry of Commerce, Thailand.

SOUTH KOREAN TRADE BARRIERS REVIEW

The success of the AKFTA depends on the success in barrier elimination. Accordingly, this section will examine the barriers that must be eliminated.

Import Policies

Tariff Barriers

South Korea has a relatively low average weighted tariff rate of 4.5 per cent for industrial products. However, the average weighted tariff for agricultural products stands at 64.1 per cent. The high tariff rate on agricultural products is a significant barrier for ASEAN agricultural products. However, tariffs on most forestry and fishery products are not bound to the high rate.

South Korea imposes tariff rates of 30 per cent or higher on most fruits and nuts, many fresh vegetables, starches, peanuts, peanut butter, various vegetable oils, juices, jams, beer, and some dairy products. In many instances, South Korea applies high tariffs despite the absence of domestic production.

In addition, South Korea has established tariff-rate quotas (TRQs) that are intended to provide minimum access to previously closed markets. In-quota tariff rates are either at 0 per cent or very low, but the over-quota tariff rates for some products are very high. For example, natural and artificial honey are subject to an over-quota tariff rate of 243 per cent; skim and whole milk powder, 176 per cent; and popcorn, 630 per cent.

In order to protect domestic agricultural producers, South Korea uses adjustment tariffs and compounded taxes to boost applied tariff rates. Most of the adjustment tariffs are imposed on agricultural and seafood products, which are of interest to the ASEAN exporters. In 2004 South Korea eliminated adjustment tariffs on three textile products, namely silk yarn, woven silk fabrics, and woven cotton gauze fabrics; it renewed adjustment tariffs on nineteen items, and reduced the tariff rates for seven of these nineteen items. In 2005 South Korea eliminated adjustment tariffs on frozen squid, renewed adjustment tariffs on ten products, and lowered adjustment tariffs on eight products.

South Korea, through its Uruguay Round commitments, has also reduced bound tariffs to zero on most or all products in the following sectors: paper, toys, steel, furniture, semiconductors, and farm equipment. South Korea has harmonized and bound most of its tariffs on textile and apparel products at the following levels: 13 to 16 per cent for man-made fibres and yarns, 30 per cent for fabrics and made-up goods, and 35 per cent for apparel.

Non-Tariff Barriers

As part of its commitments to the WTO Agreement on Agriculture, South Korea agreed to reduce its domestic support or Aggregate Measurement of Support (AMS) for agricultural products by 13 per cent in 2004. However, the level of domestic support for the cattle industry has been increasing. The United States and Australia have raised the issue as to whether South Korea's domestic support is in line with its WTO commitments on domestic subsidies.

Some agricultural and fishery products face import restrictions such as quotas or TRQs with prohibitive out-of-quota tariffs. South Korea implements quantitative restrictions through its import licensing system. It also restricts imports of value-added soybean and corn products, such as popcorn and soy flakes.

According to the Uruguay Round commitments, South Korea received a ten-year exception to tariffs on rice imports, and instead negotiated a minimum market access (MMA) quota. Under the MMA quota, South Korea's rice imports grew over ten years from 0 to 4 per cent of domestic consumption. The South Korean state trading enterprises have full control over the purchase, distribution, and end-use of imported rice. Most of the imported rice comes from China. Despite the fact that the MMA arrangement expired at the end of 2004, South Korea has exercised its rights to negotiate with WTO rice-exporting countries to seek an additional ten-year extension. Under the extension, South Korea would double its total rice imports over the next ten years to 8 per cent of domestic consumption without the control by the state enterprises.

Export Subsidies

South Korea is committed to phasing out export subsidy programmes that are not permitted under the WTO Agreement on Subsidies and Countervailing

Measures. Traditionally, the South Korean Government has provided financial assistance to exporting firms, such as low-cost facility investment loans and loan guarantees, tax benefits for facility expansion, and government sale of debt obligations.

Services Barriers

South Korea continues to maintain restrictions on some services sectors. In these sectors foreign investment is prohibited or severely circumscribed through equity or other restrictions.

South Korea stipulates that domestic films be shown in each cinema for a minimum number of days per year (146 days with reduction to 106 days possible if certain criteria are met). In 2004 the market share of South Korean films was 57 per cent. Foreign activities in the free television sector are limited to 20 per cent. Annual quotas also limit broadcasts of foreign programming to a maximum of 75 per cent for motion pictures, 55 per cent for animation, and 40 per cent for popular music. Foreign investment is not permitted for terrestrial television operations.

South Korea restricts the establishment of foreign accounting firms, as its laws stipulate that companies must employ at least ten Koreans, at least three of whom must be partners and seven of whom must be certified accountants.

In the financial sector South Korea has agreed to bind its Organization for Economic Co-operation and Development (OECD) commitments on financial services market access in the WTO. However, South Korea continues to place some restrictions to limit foreign bank activities, such as limitation on loans to individual customers, foreign exchange trading, and foreign-bank capital adequacy and liquidity requirements.

Investment Barriers

South Korea continues to promote a more favourable investment climate to facilitate foreign investment in the country. However, two sectors (television and radio stations) remain fully closed to FDI and twenty-seven sectors remain partially closed. The government still maintains foreign equity restrictions with respect to investment in various state-owned firms and many types of media, including basic telecommunication services, cable and satellite television and channel services, schools, and beef wholesaling. Foreigners still cannot produce certain agricultural products for commercial purposes and are forbidden to remove agriculturally zoned land from agricultural production.

ASEAN TRADE BARRIERS REVIEW:
THE CASE OF THAILAND

Import Policies

Thailand continues to use its high tariff structure to protect domestic products. The country's average applied tariff rate is 16 per cent. Its highest tariff rates apply to imports competing with locally produced goods, including agricultural products, automobiles and parts, alcoholic beverages, and fabrics. After the 1997–98 financial crisis Thailand increased its duties, surcharges, and excise taxes on luxury products, including wine, passenger cars, and wool carpets. Thailand has also imposed a 60 per cent duty on motorcycles.

To protect the agricultural sector, Thailand has imposed high tariffs on several agricultural products, including meats, fresh winter fruits, and winter vegetables. This means that even food produce from Thailand is limited. Import duties on agricultural and processed food are as high as 55 per cent, and the average tariff rate is 29.6 per cent.

South Korea may be interested in exporting automobiles to Thailand. However, import duties and taxes in the Thai automotive sector are among the highest in Asia. Tariffs on passenger cars and sport utility vehicles are 80 per cent and on parts and components range from 40 to 60 per cent. The tariffs on raw materials for part production are 35 per cent.

Thailand's tariff rates for textiles are also high, ranging from 25 to 40 per cent for fabrics, 10 to 25 per cent for yarns, and 35 to 45 per cent for apparel.

Thailand still utilizes the import-licence system. Import licences are required for at least twenty-six items, including many raw materials, petroleum, industrial materials, textiles, pharmaceuticals, and agricultural items. Imports of used motorcycles and parts and gaming machines are prohibited. Some items, such as certain minerals, arms and ammunition, and art objects, require special permits from government agencies.

Government Procurement

Government procurement is an area that is of interest to South Korean concerns. Thailand is not a signatory to the WTO Agreement on Government Procurement. While non-discriminatory treatment and open competition to all potential bidder policies are applied, Thai state enterprises typically have their own individual procurement policies and practices. Some countries have complained that preferential treatment is provided to domestic suppliers.

Export Subsidies

Thailand offers programmes to support trade in certain manufactured products and processed agricultural products. Such programmes include tax benefits, import duty reductions, and below-market rate credit. The Thai Government also offers preferential financing for exporters in the form of packing credits.

Services Barriers

Thailand was committed under the WTO to open the telecommunications sector to foreign firms by January 2000. The market had been dominated by two operators, the Communications Authority of Thailand (CAT) and the TOT Corporation Public Company Limited.

In the banking sector foreigners are permitted to own up to 100 per cent of Thai banks and financial companies for ten years from the date of acquisition. However, foreign banks operating in Thailand are still disadvantaged as they are limited to a maximum of three branches, of which only one may be in Bangkok.

Foreigners are prohibited from participating in construction and civil engineering activities. Construction firms must be registered in Thailand. There is a nationality requirement for one to be an architect or engineer in Thailand. Foreigners also cannot be accountants in Thailand, as they cannot be licensed as certified public accountants. The foreigner who is an accountant will be limited to serving in the capacity of a business consultant.

CONCLUSION

Encouraged by the success of surging exports following its first FTA with Chile in 2004, South Korea unveiled an ambitious plan to push for FTAs with more than fifteen countries by 2007. ASEAN comprises ten countries, which collectively are South Korea's major trading partner. In 2003 ASEAN became South Korea's fifth-largest trading partner, taking 10.4 per cent of South Korea's total trade volume. An AKFTA is crucial to South Korea's access to the Southeast Asian market.

According to the agreement, the AKFTA calls for the comprehensive liberalization for trade in goods. It also covers a wide range of economic co-operation, including small and medium-sized enterprises (SMEs), customs procedures, tourism, trade and investment promotion, and capacity building. The negotiations on the AKFTA started in early 2005 and are expected to be completed within two years.

With a goal of achieving zero tariffs for 80 per cent of its products in 2009, the AKFTA still has a long way to go. Given the current trade barriers of South Korea and Thailand, both governments will continue to protect their domestic producers in several sectors, especially in the agricultural sector.

South Korea's average tariff for agricultural products is 64.1 per cent, while the Thai tariffs on agricultural products are as high as 55 per cent, with the average tariff rate at 29.6 per cent. Moreover, both countries apply TRQs for several agricultural products.

Both countries are zealously protecting their textile and apparel sectors. Thailand's applied tariff rates for textiles are at 25–40 per cent for fabrics, 10–25 per cent for yarns, and 35–45 per cent for apparel. South Korea's tariff rates are at 13–16 per cent for man-made fibres and yarns, 30 per cent for fabrics and synthetic fibres, and 35 per cent for apparel.

In the services sector South Korea continues to maintain restrictions. While Thailand has opened its services sector, it is clear that its financial sector is set to remain closed to foreigners for at least the next ten years.

With Thailand's and South Korea's trade and investment barriers, the success of the AKFTA is beyond the two-year time frame.

South Korea's shipments to Chile increased 58.7 per cent in the eleven months from a year earlier with the commencement of the bilateral FTA in April 2004. South Korea's car exports to South America have jumped 59.3 per cent, while mobile phone exports have increased 225.7 per cent, and colour television shipments 110.4 per cent. Meanwhile, South Korean imports from Chile increased 54.3 per cent during the same period, mostly raw materials, including copper ore. While these instances of economic growth bestow great benefits to Thailand and South Korea, there are some detriments as well. The unproductive sectors unable to compete with the imported products would suffer the most. With the net gain from free trade, the continuation of protection policy may have to give way.

The agricultural sector is a great concern for Thailand. After South Korea's agreement with Chile, imports of agricultural products from Chile, except wine, grew less than 3 per cent. This is a cause for concern for South Korean farmers who are protesting against the opening of the country's closed agricultural market. However, it increases the concerns of some ASEAN countries, especially those exporting more agricultural products to South Korea. If ASEAN farmers are unable to benefit from this FTA, the negotiation process may be prolonged. In order to reach the targeted agreement as planned, South Korea should express its intention on limiting non-local agricultural market access.

APPENDIX 6.1

Core Elements of the Framework Agreement for AKFTA

Coverage

1. Comprehensive liberalization and facilitation of economic relations between ASEAN and South Korea, *inter alia*, trade in goods, trade in services, and investment;
2. Identification and abolition of non-tariff barriers (NTBs), and introduction of disciplines to ensure that the NTBs do not impede trade;
3. Comprehensive range of economic co-operation, including but not limited to: SMEs, customs procedures, tourism, trade and investment promotion, capacity building;
4. Consultation and dispute settlement mechanisms on issues arising from the interpretation and application of the measures for implementing the agreement; and
5. Development of infrastructure, especially for CLMV.

Level of Liberalization

1. Substantive liberalization in all sectors, with the provision of flexibility where appropriate; and
2. Consideration of sensitivities in particular sectors and the different stages of economic development of each participating country.

Negotiation Modalities

1. Negotiation between ASEAN and South Korea as a whole; taking into account sensitivities in particular sectors and the different stages of economic development of each participating country, in particular, provision of special and differential treatment to ASEAN and additional flexibility for CLMV in the implementation of measures in the Framework Agreement; and
2. Negotiation sequencing matters: comprehensive negotiations for all three pillars — trade in goods, services, and investment, as well as economic co-operation activities.

Others

1. Conclusion of a Framework Agreement to facilitate negotiations and draw out concrete commitments from the eleven participating countries; and

2. Making efforts on the early realization of a FTA, taking into account, *inter alia*,
    (a) The accordance of most-favoured-nation (MFN) treatment, consistent with WTO rules and principles, for ASEAN countries which are non-WTO members;
    (b) The importance of economic co-operation; and
    (c) The possibility of achieving early results prior to the establishment of a free trade area, through the immediate implementation of measures mutually agreed upon in the Framework Agreement, by commencing such tariff elimination for products which are not sensitive to either side, and economic co-operation projects yielding mutual benefits.

The negotiations on the AKFTA commenced in early 2005 and should be completed within two years. The AKFTA will be realized at an earlier date, with a goal of achieving as high a level of liberalization as possible, whereby at least 80 per cent of products will have zero tariffs in 2009, and with consideration for special and differential treatment and additional flexibility for new ASEAN countries. The AKFTA will have differentiated time frames for South Korea and the ASEAN-Six on the one hand, and CLMV on the other.

APPENDIX 6.2

ASEAN FTAs and Regional Trade Agreements

ASEAN Country	WTO/APEC Member	FTA/RTA Concluded	FTA/RTA Under Negotiation	Future FTA/RTA Planned
ASEAN			ASEAN–China FTA ASEAN–India FTA ASEAN–Australia and New Zealand FTA ASEAN–Korea FTA	ASEAN–Japan FTA
Brunei Darussalam	Yes/Yes	AFTA	Trade and Investment Framework Agreement (TIFA) with the United States (2002)	
Cambodia	Yes/No	AFTA		
Indonesia	Yes/Yes	AFTA	TIFA with the United States	Japan
Lao PDR	No/No	AFTA		
Malaysia	Yes/Yes	AFTA	TIFA with the United States Japan (six rounds)	Australia New Zealand South Korea India — Comprehensive Economic Co-operation Agreement (CECA)
Myanmar	Yes/No	AFTA		
Philippines	Yes/Yes	AFTA	TIFA with the United States Japan (three rounds)	

APPENDIX 6.2 (continued)

Singapore	Yes/Yes	AFTA Australia Japan EFTA (Switzerland, Iceland, Liechtenstein, and Norway) New Zealand United States Jordan	Pacific Three (Singapore/New Zealand/Chile — two rounds) Canada (six rounds) India (five rounds) Bahrain Kuwait South Korea (completed feasibility study) Mexico (six rounds) Sri Lanka (one round) Panama Peru Qatar (one round)	Iran
Thailand	Yes/Yes	AFTA Australia Bahrain China (Preferential Trade Agreement on Agriculture, October 2003) India (effective March 2004)	United States Japan (Closer Economic Partnership) Chile Australia New Zealand Papua New Guinea Peru	EFTA (Switzerland, Iceland, Liechtenstein, and Norway) Czech Republic Croatia South Korea Canada Hong Kong Mexico (feasibility stage) South Africa (feasibility stage)
Vietnam	No/Yes	AFTA	Sri Lanka	

Sources: "Singapore Free Trade Agreements", app.fta.gov.sg; "ASEAN Speeds Up Trade Talk with Dialogue Partners", www.aseansec.org; "ASEAN–Korea Free Trade Set to Start", www.bilaterals.org; "Korea's FTA Policy", www.pecc.org; "Thailand and FTA", www.thaifta.com; "Analysis: S. Korea's FTA Push", www.washingtontimes.com; Ministry of Commerce, Thailand, www.moc.go.th.

7
Regional Trade Arrangement between ASEAN and Korea: Korea's Perspective

Yul Kwon and Innwon Park

INTRODUCTION

Until the 1997 East Asian financial crisis, Korea had been achieving successful economic growth without any concrete economic co-operation agreements with neighbouring countries. Korea had also favoured multilateral trade liberalization and voiced strong concerns about the proliferation of regionalism and its discriminatory effects. However, responding to the worldwide movement towards regionalism in the 1990s and the necessity for regional economic co-operation after the financial crisis of 1997, Korea is now showing enthusiasm for regional trade arrangements (RTAs) and actively participating in multiple negotiations with both intra- and inter-regional countries for free trade agreements (FTAs).

As a tangible example of enthusiasm for economic co-operation, Korea concluded an FTA with Chile, which went into effect in 2004. Korea signed an FTA with Singapore in August 2005 and agreed to an FTA with the European Free Trade Association (EFTA) in July 2005. Korea is independently discussing setting up bilateral FTAs with Japan, Canada, Mexico, India, and the

United States and actively participating not only in the formation of a plurilateral FTA with China and Japan, but also the signing of a multilateral agreement with ASEAN, MERCOSUR, and ASEAN plus Three.

In particular, Korea has proposed conducting a comprehensive study on closer economic relations between Korea and ASEAN and launching a meeting of experts. Over the past four decades, the relationship between ASEAN and Korea has been one of consistent growth. This success largely derives from complementary aspects on both sides. Bilateral trade and investment between Korea and ASEAN have been steadily increasing in recent decades. Even though trade volume decreased in 1998 due to the financial crisis, it recovered after 1999. Currently they are each other's fifth largest trading partner and ASEAN is the third-largest destination for foreign direct investment (FDI) from Korea.

In discussing the deepening interdependence between Korea and ASEAN, this chapter firstly deals with why Korea shifted its policy stance from supporting multilateralism to regionalism and why Korea chose ASEAN as an immediate partner to form an FTA with by carefully analysing the economic relations between the two economies in section two. In section three, we will focus on a possible FTA between ASEAN and Korea as a feasible framework for further integration. Concluding remarks follow in section four.

REGIONAL TRADE ARRANGEMENT BETWEEN ASEAN AND KOREA

Proliferating RTAs in Korea

As shown in Table 7.1, RTA negotiations are proliferating in Korea. After the outbreak of the East Asian financial crisis in 1997, Korea's commercial policy stance in favour of multilateral trade arrangements shifted to RTAs. The financial crisis spurred the demand for regional economic co-operation, which calls for more co-operation and policy co-ordination among neighbouring economies in the region. Interdependence among East Asian economies through regional trade has also increased. That is, the intra-East Asian trade share in 2000 was 48.5 per cent, compared to 46.5 per cent for intra-North American Free Trade Agreement (NAFTA) and 53.2 per cent for intra-European Union (EU). In addition, the slow progress of multilateral negotiations under the World Trade Organization (WTO) and the Asia-Pacific Economic Co-operation (APEC) encouraged the shifting preference to regionalism. Korea's regime change towards a more liberalized economic system can be counted as another important factor behind the strategic change in favour of regionalism.

From Table 7.1, we can identify several common characteristics in Korea's effort to build RTAs. First, the proliferation of RTAs has led to a fear of being left out and has driven it to having its own RTAs, from a "bandwagon" or "domino" effect.[1] Second, there has been some progress in implementing inter-regional RTAs, such as the Korea–Chile FTA and the Korea–EFTA FTA, but there has been no significant progress in forming intra-regional RTAs with the exception of the Korea–Singapore RTA. Most intra-regional RTAs involving Korea are still under negotiation or discussion. It means that Korea still has a long way to go before realizing the gains from freer trade through the formation of RTAs. Third, bilateral agreements are favoured because they are less costly and more easily open to others. In particular, for beginners to RTAs like Korea, bilateral arrangements with relatively experienced counterparts such as Singapore and Chile are expected to serve as a valuable learning process in regionalism. Fourth, low transaction costs from shared borders are no longer a critical factor for building a regional bloc. Recent innovations in information and communication technology reinforce the remarkable efficiency gains from international transactions of goods, services, and finance. In this vein Korea is very eager to make inter-RTAs with large markets like the United States and India.

Table 7.1
Proliferating RTAs in Korea

	Status	Intra-RTAs	Inter-RTAs
Bilateral RTAs			
Korea–Chile	Implemented		✓
Korea–Singapore	Signed	✓	
Korea–Japan	Under negotiation	✓	
Korea–Mexico	Joint study		✓
Korea–China	Joint study	✓	
Korea–United States	Discussion		✓
Korea–Canada	Discussion		✓
Korea–India	Discussion	✓	
Plurilateral or Multilateral RTAs			
Korea–EFTA	Signed		✓
Korea–ASEAN	Under negotiation	✓	
Korea–China–Japan	Joint study	✓	
Korea–MERCOSUR	Discussion		✓
ASEAN plus Three	Discussion	✓	

Sources: Ministry of Foreign Affairs and Trade, Korea, http://www.fta.go.kr/index.php; http://www.bilaterals.org/.

In sum, we find that the formation of RTAs can be a new engine of economic prosperity and stability for the Korean economy, and a way to avoid the recurrence of the financial crisis and revitalize its growth momentum. The gains from trade and investment liberalization expected through intra- and inter-RTAs will move the Korean economy to a more advanced level of economic development.

Economic Co-operation between ASEAN and Korea

Economic Interdependence between ASEAN and Korea: Trade and Investment[2]

Economic interdependence through trade and investment linkages between ASEAN and Korea has significantly deepened over the past few decades. In 2004 ASEAN became Korea's fifth-largest trading partner, taking 9.5 per cent of Korea's total exports, as shown in Table 7.2.

Although bilateral trade and investment between ASEAN and Korea decreased sharply during the East Asian financial crisis, economic relations between the two sides recovered rapidly. For the trade balance, Korea has recorded a constant trade surplus with a peak surplus of US$78 billion in 1997. However, since the financial crisis ASEAN's deficit has been decreasing, and the balance of trade between the two economies is moving towards equilibrium.

Table 7.2
Korea's Exports to and Imports from ASEAN
(US$ million)

	Total Exports	Exports to ASEAN	Share (%)	Total Imports	Imports from ASEAN	Share (%)
1996	129,715	20,311	15.7	150,339	12,074	8.0
1997	136,164	20,365	15.0	144,616	12,549	8.7
1998	132,313	15,328	11.6	93,282	9,135	9.8
1999	143,685	17,708	12.3	119,752	12,250	10.2
2000	172,268	20,134	11.7	160,481	18,173	11.3
2001	150,439	16,459	10.9	141,098	15,916	11.3
2002	162,471	18,400	11.3	152,126	16,757	11.0
2003	193,817	20,253	10.4	178,827	18,459	10.3
2004	253,845	24,024	9.5	224,463	22,383	10.0

Source: KOTIS (Korea International Trade Association).

ASEAN is Korea's third-largest investment destination in cumulative terms. The trend of Korean firms' FDI to ASEAN is shown in Table 7.3. Since the mid-1980s, Korean firms have looked to ASEAN countries as a source of cheap labour as well as abundant natural resources. Korean firms also exported manufactured goods produced in Southeast Asia to developed countries. Such an export platform strategy allowed these firms to bypass the trade barriers to Korean products in third-country markets.

ASEAN's share in Korea's outward FDI continuously increased from the late 1980s to 1991, but due to investment in China after the normalization of diplomatic relations between Korea and China, Korea's outward FDI towards the ASEAN region decreased until the mid-1990s. This downward trend continued after the financial crisis, excluding a sudden upward climb in 2003. Nevertheless, the amount invested in ASEAN climbed upwards again with the recent recovery of the ASEAN economy. In 2004 Korea's total investment in ASEAN reached US$501.8 million (8.5 per cent), in a total of 282 projects.

Table 7.3
Korea's FDI Outflows to ASEAN
(US$ million)

	Total Investment			Net Investment		
	Projects	Amount	Share* (%)	Projects	Amount	Share* (%)
1988	32	31.9	14.8	26	27.6	17.7
1989	69	91.6	16.0	67	90.1	22.8
1990	119	238.7	24.9	115	235.4	28.9
1991	137	330.5	29.6	132	326.2	31.7
1992	106	271.3	22.3	90	255.9	23.5
1993	106	168.3	13.3	97	150.1	14.7
1994	275	257.2	11.2	260	200.6	9.8
1995	183	605.5	19.3	155	496.6	17.5
1996	219	445.5	10.1	188	372.7	9.9
1997	173	616.3	17.1	151	531.8	15.8
1998	62	501.1	10.6	46	393.7	10.6
1999	114	464.1	14.2	99	357.1	15.5
2000	183	463.6	9.5	170	259.9	7.4
2001	192	379.8	7.4	169	−559.9	−30.7
2002	266	348.8	9.5	249	199.4	7.7
2003	232	536.8	13.5	214	480.5	14.6
2004	282	501.8	8.5	254	444.3	8.6

*ASEAN's share in Korea's outward FDI (total and net invested).
Source: Korean Export and Import Bank database.

According to Table 7.4, which analyses current trends and the cumulative state of Korean investment in ASEAN by industry, the manufacturing sector eclipses nearly all other sectors, comprising 60.1 per cent of total investment and 57.5 per cent of net investment up to 2004. Based on the total amount invested, the wholesale and retail, mining, real estate and services, telecommunications, and construction sectors follow the manufacturing sector. Note that investment in ASEAN in the telecommunications sector is on an upward trend. The net investment in the telecommunications sector in ASEAN reached US$305 million by 2004.

Table 7.5 shows the scale of Korean investment in ASEAN countries. Indonesia is the most significant FDI destination for Korea among the ASEAN countries, comprising 28.9 per cent of the investment. Vietnam is the second most favourable destination for investment with 23.5 per cent. Among the ten ASEAN members, 98 per cent of total investments are concentrated in six ASEAN countries, namely Indonesia, Vietnam, Thailand, the Philippines, Malaysia and Singapore, while only 2 per cent are in Myanmar, Cambodia, Laos, and Brunei.

ASEAN as the Right Partner

Who would be the best RTA partner to help maximize net gains? Forming an RTA with the right partner will serve as a building block towards global free trade by maximizing the trade creation effect while minimizing the trade diversion effect. Wonnacott and Lutz (1989), Summers (1991), Krugman (1993), and Frankel, Stein, and Wei (1995) introduce the concept of "natural trading partner", by arguing that certain characteristics between RTA members can maximize the positive welfare gains from RTAs. They find that with larger pre-RTA trade volumes and lower transportation costs between members, RTAs are more likely to be welfare-improving. More specifically, Wonnacott and Lutz (1989) and De Melo, Panagariya, and Rodrik (1993) list the factors that create larger net gains from an RTA as follows: (1) higher initial tariff on a given sector creates larger net gains, (2) lower post-RTA external tariffs are less likely to create a trade diversion effect, and (3) greater complementarity between members induces larger net gains. The larger pre-RTA intra-regional trade volume between members is another important factor in creating larger gains from an RTA.

Is ASEAN a natural trading partner with whom the Korean economy can maximize net gains through an RTA? An RTA between ASEAN and Korea would incorporate many characteristics potentially capable of generating trade creation effects to overwhelm trade diversion effects. The high

Table 7.4
Korea's FDI in ASEAN by Industry
(US$ thousand)

Sector	2001	2002	2003	2004	Total Investment	Net Investment
Agriculture*	772	592	1,247	1,435	73,453 (1.1%)	47,729 (1.1%)
Mining	11,013	23,334	114,130	104,663	689,170 (10.6%)	628,954 (14.0%)
Manufacturing	267,681	205,752	132,944	217,734	3,905,328 (60.1%)	2,579,475 (57.5%)
Construction	33,032	11,519	10,833	11,906	243,550 (3.8%)	171,904 (3.8%)
Wholesale/Retail	27,774	14,789	200,581	23,108	680,524 (10.5%)	249,419 (5.6%)
Storage	954	2,573	1,594	10,967	32,711 (0.5%)	27,115 (0.6%)
Telecommunications	274	11,328	37,283	75,839	322,890 (5.0%)	305,000 (6.8%)
Finance/Insurance	5	0	0	0	455 (0.0%)	455 (0.0%)
Hotels/Restaurants	1,135	719	640	5,332	77,705 (1.2%)	50,691 (1.1%)
Real estate/Services	30,143	46,621	8,752	52,104	467,820 (7.2%)	428,223 (9.5%)
Others	0	54	0	0	54 (0.0%)	54 (0.0%)

*Forestry and fishery are included under the agriculture sector.
Source: Korean Export and Import Bank database.

Table 7.5
Korea's FDI in ASEAN by Country
(US$ thousand)

Country	2001	2002	2003	2004	Total Investment
Malaysia	19,872	6,189	6,428	35,997	370,281 (8.3%)
Thailand	30,777	31,480	26,496	44,896	573,354 (12.8%)
Indonesia	169,480	64,728	78,528	56,361	1,294,345 (28.9%)
Singapore	40,918	48,166	234,343	164,023	586,821 (13.1%)
Philippines	56,933	26,732	16,363	13,764	514,138 (11.5%)
Vietnam	46,280	135,403	136,512	172,426	1,053,248 (23.5%)
Cambodia	5,540	3,877	9,219	13,531	48,149 (1.1%)
Myanmar	2,948	660	0	0	29,678 (0.7%)
Laos	35	50	115	2,090	9,180 (0.2%)
Brunei	0	0	0	0	1,937 (0.0%)

Source: Korean Export and Import Bank database.

Table 7.6
Average Tariff Rates in Korea and Major ASEAN Countries
(In percentages)

	1988	1993	1996	1998	2000
Korea	18.1	8.9	7.9	7.9	7.9
Singapore	0.3	0.4	0.0	0.0	0.0
Malaysia	13.6	12.8	9.0	9.3	9.2
Thailand	31.2	37.8	17.0	18.4	17.0
Indonesia	18.1	17.0	13.1	11.9	8.2
Philippines	27.9	23.5	14.0	9.4	6.9

Source: Lee and Park (2005).

pre-RTA trade shares in Table 7.2 and non-uniform tariff structures in ASEAN countries and Korea (see Table 7.6) can serve as additional factors behind the expectation of a stronger trade creation effect. Moreover, with their participation in many rounds of multilateral trade arrangements under the General Agreement on Tariffs and Trade (GATT), they have already lowered external tariffs against non-members, as shown in Table 7.6. This may reduce the problem of incurring a trade diversion effect. It is also expected that an RTA between ASEAN and Korea would strongly influence other East Asian countries, such as Japan and China, to move faster towards a more integrated East Asian economy such as ASEAN plus Three or an East Asian Free Trade Area (EAFTA).

Does complementarity matter? Is it better for a group of countries which have complementary pre-RTA trade structures to form an RTA? De Melo, Panagariya, and Rodrik (1993) list greater complementarity in import demands of members as one of the factors that create larger gains from an FTA. They also emphasize geographical proximity as an important but not dominant consideration in forming a trade bloc. Baldwin and Venables (1995) argue that RTAs do not necessarily contract external trade if complementarities between goods traded internally lead to an increase in external trade. By looking not only at the trade volume created but also at the gains for each dollar of new trade created, Wonnacott and Lutz (1989) explain that complementarity is desirable in order to make larger gains per unit of trade creation and incur smaller costs per unit of trade diversion if the member countries' costs of production are close to the world average. Elliott and Ikemoto (2003) estimate a Gravity equation with a complementarity index and support the hypothesis that the larger trade creation effect is possible in the case of an ASEAN FTA, when a pair of bloc members has complementary endowments that is "reflected in the structure of the commodities traded". As indicated in Table 7.7, complementarity in the trade structure between ASEAN and Korea is another important factor as to why Korea chose ASEAN as a partner with whom to maximize gains from freer trade.

Considering the fast-growing ASEAN economy in which cheap labour, abundant natural resources, and potential local markets can be utilized, an ASEAN–Korea RTA would surely create bigger dynamic gains from freer trade. In addition, co-operation with ASEAN would provide better security and political stability in the region that may attract more FDI.

Overall, we find strong incentives for Korea to direct its trade liberalization efforts towards ASEAN. For Korea, ASEAN is a very attractive partner with whom to maximize gains from freer trade and investment. In addition to the traditional gains from free trade, Korea will benefit from ASEAN's experience, pre-existing rules, and readiness of negotiation tables. Moreover, ASEAN may be able to assume a mediating role in alleviating leadership competition and political tension between China and Japan in East Asia.

AN ASEAN–KOREA FREE TRADE AGREEMENT

As we discussed earlier in detail, ASEAN is one of the most feasible and suitable partners among Korea's several potential RTA partners. Currently, ASEAN and Korea are aiming to achieve an agreement to establish an FTA between them for trade in the commodity sector by the end of 2005, for

Table 7.7
Complementarity between ASEAN and Korea in 2003
(US$ thousand)

| | ASEAN's Exports to Korea by Product | | | | ASEAN's Imports from Korea by Product | | |
HS Code	Commodity Item	Export Value	Share (%)	HS Code	Commodity Item	Import Value	Share (%)
84–85	Machinery and electrical appliances	7,979,970	43.2	84–85	Machinery and electrical appliances	10,501,464	51.9
24–27	Mineral products	5,312,059	28.8	50–63	Textiles and apparel	1,908,313	9.4
28–38	Chemicals	841,028	4.6	72–83	Base metal and metal articles	1,837,489	9.1
39–40	Plastics	597,091	3.2	28–38	Chemicals	1,159,079	5.7
44–46	Wood and wood articles	592,216	3.2	39–40	Plastics	1,111,735	5.5
	Total	18,458,465	100		Total	20,253,388	100

Source: Kwon (2004).

trade in services by the end of 2006, and to completely implement an ASEAN–Korea FTA (AKFTA) in 2009. Table 7.8 summarizes the chronological events of bilateral talks between ASEAN and Korea for an AKFTA. As we can see from the table, Korea is expected to conclude FTA negotiations with ASEAN within the year as the fifth round of FTA talks held in Seoul on 6–9 September 2005 between the two sides showed significant progress. According to the draft, Korea and ASEAN agreed to liberalize about 90 per cent of the goods in trade.

If the AKFTA is realized and implemented, the FTA would cover a combined population of 584 million and a combined GDP of US$1.07 trillion. According to Korean Institute for International Economic Policy (KIEP) estimates using a traditional Computable General Equilibrium (CGE) Model Analysis, the possible AKFTA is expected to boost ASEAN's GDP by 0.41 per cent and Korea's GDP by 0.13 per cent.

CONCLUDING REMARKS

In order to revitalize its engine of economic growth in a globalizing world economy, Korea has shifted its commercial policy stance from supporting multilateralism to favouring regionalism. Korea has already made some progress in this direction, as can be seen by the Korea–Chile FTA, the Korea–Singapore FTA, and the Korea–EFTA FTA. In addition, Korea is currently attempting to form multiple FTAs with intra- and inter-regional economies, including ASEAN. This chapter briefly highlighted the deepening interdependence and emerging need for economic co-operation between ASEAN and Korea, and emphasized why Korea chose ASEAN as the best partner for a possible FTA to maximize gains from freer trade and investment.

As tangible evidence of their co-operative efforts, ASEAN and Korea have made substantial progress in their negotiations on an FTA, including customs clearance and dispute settlement, laying a basis particularly for the conclusion of an agreement on the liberalization of commodities by the end of 2005 as originally planned at the fifth FTA meeting between ASEAN and Korea on 6–9 September 2005 in Seoul.

It is important that any co-operation plan between the two sides should focus not only on maximizing economic gains through liberalized economic activities but also provide a broad understanding for a new plan for ASEAN–Korea co-operation. In particular, an appropriate and flexible time frame for a possible FTA should be considered, taking into account the economic levels and sensitive sectors on both sides. Deeper integration is another important ingredient both Korea and ASEAN should consider. As Lee and Park (2005)

Table 7.8

Chronology of Major Talks between ASEAN and Korea for an AKFTA

Date	Contents
8 October 2003	At the ASEAN–Korea summit in Bali, Indonesia, leaders of both sides tasked their ministers with discussing the possibility of establishing an FTA and launching a joint study for the comprehensive enhancement of economic relations, including an FTA.
13 February 2004	At the first consultation between ASEAN Senior Economic Officials and Korea in Siemreap, Cambodia, both sides agreed to the terms of reference regarding the operation of an ASEAN–Korea Experts Group (ASEAN–Korea EG).
8–9 March 2004	The first meeting of the ASEAN–Korea EG at the ASEAN Secretariat in Jakarta, Indonesia: Both sides exchanged opinions on issues of focus for future experts' meetings, such as the scope of application of the FTA negotiations, negotiation modalities, procedures, and timetables for drafting the joint report.
16–17 April 2004	The second meeting of the ASEAN–Korea EG at the Ministry of Foreign Affairs and Trade in Seoul, Korea: Both sides exchanged views on the current status of trade and investment between them, possibilities for liberalization in the respective sectors and anticipated effects, directions for the enhancement of bilateral economic co-operation, and future work plans.
10–11 June 2004	The third meeting of the ASEAN–Korea EG in Singapore: Both sides continued with discussions on measures for enhancing bilateral economic co-operation, especially in the areas of tourism, natural resources, education, etc. Economic experts on both sides had in-depth discussions on effective methods for analysing the economic effects of an AKFTA.
9–10 July 2004	The fourth meeting of the ASEAN–Korea EG in Seoul, Korea: Both sides reviewed the draft of the final report which contained methods for analysing Korea's and ASEAN's present economic condition; methods for liberalizing and facilitating trade; and methods for strengthening economic co-operation.
27–28 August 2004	The fifth meeting of the ASEAN–Korea EG in Jakarta, Indonesia: Both sides reached the conclusion that elimination of tariffs (excluding sensitive products) and liberalization of services and investment were needed. The Experts Group Meeting decided to submit a report that recommended the promotion of an AKFTA.

Table 7.8 *(continued)*

4 September 2004	At the ASEAN–Korea Economic Ministers' Meeting in Jakarta, Indonesia, the final report by the ASEAN–Korea EG was reviewed and declared ready for submission at the ASEAN–Korea summit meeting in November to initiate official FTA negotiations based on this report.
30 November 2004	At the eighth ASEAN–Korea summit in Vientiane, Laos, leaders on both sides welcomed the recommendations from the ASEAN–Korea EG on the measures to expand two-way trade and investment by liberalizing and integrating the markets. They affirmed that the establishment of an AKFTA would be mutually beneficial. In this regard, they agreed to launch AKFTA negotiations in early 2005 with the goal of having zero tariff for at least 80 per cent of products by 2009, and with consideration for special and differential treatment and additional flexibility for new ASEAN countries.
23–25 February 2005	The first round of official negotiations for an AKFTA in Jakarta, Indonesia.
19–21 April 2005	The second round of official negotiations for an AKFTA in Seoul, Korea.
8–10 June 2005	The third round of official negotiations for an AKFTA in Singapore.
19–20 July 2005	The fourth round of official negotiations for an AKFTA in Bangkok, Thailand.
6–9 September 2005	The fifth round of official negotiations for an AKFTA in Seoul, Korea. Both sides reached an agreement on the framework agreement, the agreement for goods in trade, customs procedures, and dispute settlement procedures. The two sides arrived at a substantial agreement on the main text of the agreement for goods in trade and established the basis for concluding an agreement on goods liberalization within the year as planned. The two sides still showed a difference in views on the range of goods and the specific time for their liberalization, the ways to protect sensitive items and also on some rules of origin, and agreed to hold future negotiations focusing on these areas.

Sources: Ministry of Foreign Affairs and Trade, Korea, http://www.mofat.go.kr/; ASEAN Secretariat, http://www.aseansec.org/4919.htm.

indicate, the movement of potential member countries towards RTAs has been motivated by the desire to enhance regional economic co-operation by facilitating trade and investment and providing a more flexible environment for the operations of multinational firms, rather than by removing grounds for discrimination and boosting intra-bloc trade through the traditional way of eliminating tariffs. The preference for deeper integration and following reform measures surely support the positive aspect of "new regionalism",[3] and may further substantiate the "domino theory of regionalism". Then, Korea's FTA with ASEAN could eventually expand into an FTA encompassing all of East Asia in the future and overcome the recent global regionalism trend.

NOTES

This chapter was completed before the signing of a Korea-ASEAN FTA. Korea and nine ASEAN members, excluding Thailand, signed an FTA on goods on 16 May 2006 as part of plans for a deeper integration.

1. See Baldwin (1993).
2. For more detailed information, see Kwon (2004).
3. See Ethier (1998).

REFERENCES

Baldwin, R. and A. Venables. "Regional Economic Integration". In *Handbook of International Economics*, edited by G. Grossman and K. Rogoff. Amsterdam: Elsevier Science Publishers, 1995.

Baldwin, Richard. "A Domino Theory of Regionalism". NBER Working Paper Series, no. 4465. National Bureau of Economic Research, 1993.

De Melo, Jaime, Arvind Panagariya, and David Rodrik. "The New Regionalism: A Country Perspective". In *New Dimensions in Regional Integration,* edited by Jaime De Melo and Arvind Panagariya, pp. 159–93. Cambridge: Centre for Economic Policy Research (CEPR), Cambridge University Press, 1993.

Elliott, Robert and Kengo Ikemoto. "AFTA and the Asian Crisis: Help or Hindrance to ASEAN Intra-Regional Trade?". The School of Economics Discussion Paper Series, no. 0311. Manchester: University of Manchester, 2003.

Ethier, Wilfred J. "The New Regionalism". *The Economic Journal* 108 (1998): 1149–61.

Frankel, Jeffrey, Ernesto Stein, and Shang-jin Wei. "Trading Blocs and the Americas: The Natural, the Unnatural, and the Super-natural". *Journal of Development Economics* 47 (1995): 61–95.

Krugman, Paul. "Regionalism versus Multilateralism: Analytical Notes". In *New Dimensions in Regional Integration*, edited by Jaime De Melo and Arvind Panagariya, pp. 58–79. Cambridge: Centre for Economic Policy Research (CEPR), Cambridge University Press, 1993.

Kwon, Yul. "Toward a Comprehensive Partnership: ASEAN–Korea Economic Cooperation". *East Asian Review* 16, no. 4 (2004): 81–98.

Lee, Jong-Wha and Innwon Park. "Free Trade Areas in East Asia: Discriminatory or Nondiscriminatory?". *The World Economy* 28, no. 1 (2005): 21–48.

Summers, Lawrence. "Regionalism and the World Trading System". Federal Reserve Bank of Kansas City, 1991.

Wonnacott, Paul and Mark Lutz. "Is There a Case for Free Trade Areas?". In *Free Trade Areas and U.S. Trade Policy*, edited by Jeffrey J. Schott, pp. 59–84. Washington, D.C.: Institute for International Economics, 1989.

Others

Korean Export and Import Bank database.
KOTIS (Korea International Trade Association).
http://www.fta.go.kr/index.php.
http://www.bilaterals.org/.
http://www.mofat.go.kr/.
http://www.aseansec.org/4919.htm.

PART IV

ASEAN–Korea Co-operation in the Development of New ASEAN Members

8

ASEAN–Korea Co-operation in the Development of New ASEAN Members

Le Dinh Tinh

INTRODUCTION

The fact that the Republic of Korea (ROK) and the Association of Southeast Asian Nations (ASEAN) officially became Dialogue Partners at the Twenty-fourth ASEAN Ministerial Meeting (AMM) in Kuala Lumpur in July 1991 did not surprise regional commentators. It had been widely known that no effort was spared to gear this bilateral relationship onto higher planes. Many researchers, including Kwon Yul, state that this relationship has witnessed consistent growth over the past four decades.[1] It should also be noted that this success "largely derives from the complementarities between both sides".[2]

There are undoubtedly common interests and potentials for further development between Korea and ASEAN. More importantly, Korea–ASEAN co-operation has led to the adoption of an inclusive approach, which attaches importance to the development of the new members of ASEAN, namely Cambodia, Laos, Myanmar, and Vietnam (CLMV for short). This chapter argues that such an approach is not only beneficial to the new members of ASEAN, the other ASEAN members, and Korea, but also East Asia as a whole.

IS ASEAN A RELEVANT PARTNER?

The ASEAN leaders' summit in Bali in October 2003 reaffirmed the commitment to establish by 2020 an ASEAN community consisting of three pillars: the ASEAN Economic Community, the ASEAN Security Community, and the ASEAN Socio-Cultural Community. ASEAN is known all over the world for its care of its member countries without which ASEAN would not have accomplished its achievements of the past thirty-eight years. In the economic sphere, economies of scale provided the rationale behind the ASEAN embrace of all Southeast Asian countries into its fold. All together ASEAN has a combined population of more than 520 million, a total GDP of over US$680 billion. The ASEAN Free Trade Area (AFTA) was set in motion twelve years ago and the more developed ASEAN economies have decided to reduce the tariff level in goods from 5 to 0 per cent. Many had thought that the admission of CLMV into ASEAN would slow down the AFTA process. However, ASEAN became stronger as a single market and a single production base, thereby fulfilling ASEAN's ultimate economic goal. Furthermore, the complementarities between ASEAN economies have been empirically proven.[3] There are programmes such as the ASEAN Investment Area (AIA) that tap into "the various complementary advantages of ASEAN member countries in order to maximize business and production efficiency at lower costs".[4]

Notwithstanding the economic crisis in 1997, ASEAN represents one of the most dynamic economic regions in the world.

ASEAN capability should include, among other things, ASEAN solidarity, which is not only reflected in intra-regional trade and investment but also in taking an outward-looking stance *vis-à-vis* globalization. In this respect, the co-operation between Korea and ASEAN is of great significance. As ASEAN Secretary-General Ong Keng Yong put it, "another key strategy ASEAN is pursuing is the strengthening of linkages with the world economy through increased trade and economic ties with ASEAN's major trade partners like China, India, Japan, and the Republic of Korea".[5] Therefore, the co-operation between Korea and ASEAN, including that between Korea and CLMV, is very important to ASEAN efforts in expanding the market, obtaining better sources of capital and intermediate products, and promoting inter-regional investment links.

Against that background, the introduction of an East Asia Community is more meaningful as it increases the social and discursive interaction, and strengthens the material links among East Asian countries. It is, therefore, in the interests of both Korea and ASEAN to support the new ASEAN countries' bid in catching up with the regional integration train which is bigger and faster. As for CLMV, it is proven that their political will to making positive contributions to the development of the region could be attributed to the growing sense of regionalism. Slowing down the region's integration train goes against the interests of all countries. Moreover, economic growth rates of CLMV (unfortunately with the exception of Myanmar) have appreciated in the past ten years.

WHAT CAN KOREA OFFER?

Korea took part in a summit meeting with ASEAN for the first time in December 1997 on the occasion of the thirtieth anniversary of the founding of ASEAN. Since then, the relationship between Korea and ASEAN has witnessed increasing development. It is recognized that Korea has been proactive in the co-operation process. In 1998, for instance, Korea proposed the creation of the East Asia Vision Group (EAVG). Similarly, between 1998 and 2002 Korea was consistently serious and committed to this proposal. The final report of the EAVG proposal was submitted at the sixth summit meeting in November 2002.

ASEAN's nominal GDP is slightly higher than Korea's (US$686.3 billion and US$605 billion respectively). However, their comparative GDP per capita differs greatly: US$1,268 and US$12,634 (approximately equivalent to 10 per cent). The differences are much more telling when CLMV's figures are compared to Korea's.[6]

It is thus reasonable to argue that the ASEAN countries, particularly CLMV, are in great need of assistance in improving the capabilities of people and institutions because this is an area where Korea enjoys formidable advantages.

As a developed country, Korea is definitely in a good position to help with narrowing the development gap within ASEAN (see more discussion below).

Besides, Korea and ASEAN could, through multilateral forums such as ASEAN plus Three and the Asia–Europe Meeting (ASEM), complement each other's interests. The ASEAN plus Three framework is, for instance, "one of the most important frameworks that advocates East Asian regionalism".[7] For countries like Vietnam, a foreign policy of openness and integration has proven beneficial to the course of national development. This integration process includes, among other things, participation in regional institutions such as ASEAN plus Three. Beyond the Asia-Pacific region, "ASEAN and Korea, as Asian partners, share many common interests in the ASEM context. In this regard, the ASEAN plus Three meeting will give opportunities for the Asian side to form a common front on many ASEM issues".[8]

NARROWING THE DEVELOPMENT GAP

The Joint Declaration on Comprehensive Co-operation Partnership between ASEAN and Korea concluded in Vientiane on 30 November 2004 is an important testimony to the fact that this substantial bilateral relationship has garnered critical momentum. There is no doubt that the declaration resulted from an increasingly mature process of mutual co-operation.

In addition to recognizing the role of Korea–ASEAN co-operation in maintaining the region's peace, stability, and security, the declaration acknowledges both sides' contribution to narrowing the development gap among ASEAN countries.[9]

Specifically, the declaration stated that both ASEAN and Korea should do the following to narrow the development gap within ASEAN:

- Strengthen co-operation and support for the realization of ASEAN integration objectives by implementing projects furthering the Bali Concord II, Initiatives for ASEAN Integration (IAI) as well as the Vientiane Action Programme (VAP), including providing technical assistance and capacity-building for the least developed countries (LDC) of ASEAN based on the experience and expertise of Korea in development.
- Strengthen ASEAN's integration efforts in narrowing the development gap within ASEAN and between ASEAN and Korea by enhancing regional and sub-regional development, including through the Mekong Sub-region, Ayeyawady–Chao Phraya–Mekong Economic Co-operation Strategy (ACMECS), the Brunei Darussalam–Indonesia–Malaysia–Philippines East ASEAN Growth Area (BIMP-EAGA), the Greater Mekong Sub-region (GMS) programme, the Second East–West Economic Corridor, the Singapore–Kunming Rail Link (SKRL) project as well as sharing experiences with the Mekong River Commission (MRC) in formulating and implementing priority programmes in the Mekong River Basin.
- Pursue and enhance co-operation in the areas of energy and resources, finance, transportation, labour, science and technology, and ICT, to narrow the digital divide and develop human resources.
- Reduce disparities and poverty by creating a supportive environment for intra-regional trade and by promoting human resources development and enhancing institutional capacity-building.
- Develop the ASEAN grass-roots economies by promoting commerce and retail activities at the local community level, improving indigenous knowledge, and developing and strengthening small and medium-sized enterprises (SMEs) to enhance the self-sufficiency and viability of the domestic economy.

On the implementation side, Korea has pledged US$5 million and has taken up five IAI projects in the areas of ICT, capacity-building in trade in goods and services, e-government and undertaking a feasibility study for the missing links and spur links of the SKRL project in CLMV.[10]

Official Development Assistance (ODA) constitutes another important source of financial support that could narrow the development gap. This is more so given the fact that

> the main portion of Korea's ODA is directed towards several ASEAN members. This is a reflection of Korea's strong desire to improve relations with ASEAN members. Korea uses its Economic Development Cooperation Fund (EDCF) to implement much of its ODA while the Korea International Cooperation Agency (KOICA) is another useful vehicle for ODA. KOICA's financial assistance has been mainly directed towards Vietnam, Indonesia, Cambodia, and Laos.[11]

Let us take another example of how Korea could extend its co-operation towards ASEAN in terms of capacity-building. The recent introduction and application of high-technology facilities at the Korean parliament reveals that Korea is well capable of further assisting CLMV in acquiring new technologies and implementing e-government.

Several lawmakers from Korea also attended the Twenty-fifth General Assembly of the ASEAN Inter-Parliamentary Organization (AIPO) from 13–16 September 2004 in Phnom Penh, Cambodia, where ASEAN lawmakers urged richer ASEAN countries to help the new members to improve farm productivity through scientific co-operation and human resources development, and improved access to and exchanging knowledge on modern techniques of agricultural production.

In tandem with the efforts made by the more developed countries within ASEAN in narrowing the development gap, Korea's co-operation with ASEAN should be regarded in a positive light.

However, there is room for improvement in the co-operation between Korea and ASEAN in narrowing the development gap with ASEAN. At this point, proponents of such an argument might remain devoid of empirical evidence. However, it is safe to conclude that the 2004 summit in Vientiane serves as a promising kick-off to the implementation of the scheme to narrow the development gap with the ASEAN countries. Reality calls for more deeds than words. For instance, to further "complement the ASEAN members' desire to develop more value-added industries", Korean overseas direct investment patterns could "change from labor-intensive sectors to capital and technology-intensive sectors".[12]

THE FTA

To illustrate the substantiality of ASEAN–Korea co-operation in the development of the new ASEAN members, I shall use the example of a free trade agreement (FTA).

> In discussing the FTA ASEAN–Korea Experts Group recommends consideration for special and differential treatment for the developing countries of ASEAN and additional flexibility for the newer ASEAN member countries, namely Cambodia, Laos, Myanmar and Vietnam (CLMV). The CLMV countries would be given an additional five years to realise the FTA.[13]

If Korea and ASEAN are to achieve a comprehensive economic partnership (CEP), Hank Lim suggests that both parties need to discuss and negotiate a broad range of issues, including a free trade area. In other words, a free trade area is an element of a CEP. A CEP is expected to cover the diverse economic interests of ASEAN economies, both in CLMV and the six more developed members. For instance, while CLMV might need more ODA, the ASEAN-Six are looking at a global partnership with Korea.[14]

There are two big questions that need addressing with regard to Korea–ASEAN co-operation in the development of the new members and that is related to the FTA issue. One is the question of *competitiveness vs. inclusiveness*. Economic co-operation between Korea and ASEAN of course should demand ASEAN industrial competitiveness. Therefore, the present issue is how Korea and ASEAN will solve the seemingly contradictory goals of competitiveness and inclusiveness. It is argued that economics in ASEAN is a marathon process, a strategic trend, "not so much a matter of policy".[15] It simply adopts a long-term vision addressing all issues. It cannot be denied that ASEAN has efficiently prioritized its development agenda. It is, however, noteworthy that the prioritization and inclusion of development items are not mutually exclusive in the long run.

The other issue is *bilateralism vs. multilateralism*. Many have adopted the view that bilateral co-operation between Korea and an individual ASEAN country is an integral part of Korea–ASEAN partnership. For example, bilateral FTAs between Korea and ASEAN should be designed in a way that is conducive to region-wide trade liberalization. Thus the complications deriving from an emphasis on the bilateral approach to Korea–ASEAN co-operation could be solved if certain conditions are met. Hank Lim suggests that bilateral trade partnership could help promote regional and multilateral trade and investment if it abides by the principles of openness and non-discrimination.[16] In this sense, it would be a compelling argument if the whole region is interconnected by open and outward-looking mechanisms.

CONCLUSIONS

We are living in a world where co-operation for the sake of achieving inclusive development is always positive. Korea–ASEAN co-operation has been directed towards that worthy goal. The Joint Declaration recorded in Vientiane in 2004 serves as an important springboard for further intensification of relationship between Korea and ASEAN, including (but not limited to) co-operation in the development of the new members. Ranging from ODA and development gap narrowing programmes to co-ordinated multilateral endeavours such as ASEAN plus Three, ASEM, and the East Asia Community, Korea–ASEAN co-operation has seen steady progress. As such, the future ought to be bright for both parties.

NOTES

1. Kwon Yul, "Toward a Comprehensive Partnership: ASEAN–Korea Economic Cooperation", *East Asia Review* 16, no. 4 (Winter 2004): 81.
2. Ibid., p. 81.
3. See, for instance, *ASEAN Statistical Yearbook 2004* at <http://www.aseansec.org/syb2004.htm>.
4. Ong Keng Yong, Secretary-General of ASEAN, "Competitiveness: The ASEAN Way" (Keynote Address to Global Entrepolis @ Singapore, Singapore, 11 October 2004).
5. Ong Keng Yong, Secretary-General of ASEAN, "Integrating Southeast Asian Economies: Challenges for ASEAN" (Remarks at the ASEAN Energy Business Forum 2004, Manila, Philippines, 8 June 2004).
6. The total GDP and GDP per capita of Vietnam are, for instance, US$39 billion and US$480 respectively.
7. Sanae Suzuki, "Chairmanship in ASEAN+3: A Shared Rule of Behavior", Discussion Paper no. 9 (Tokyo: Institute of Developing Economies, October 2004), p. 1.
8. Inkyo Cheong, *ASEAN–Korea Cooperation in the 21st Century* (Seoul: Korea Institute for International Economic Policy (KIEP), May 2002), p. 11.
9. The Joint Declaration on Comprehensive Co-operation Partnership between the Association of Southeast Asian Nations and the Republic of Korea, 30 November 2004.
10. Cheong, op. cit., p.11.
11. Cheong, op. cit., p. 11.
12. Cheong, op. cit., p. 15.
13. ASEAN Secretariat, http://www.aseansec.org/7672.htm, last accessed on 29 August 2005.
14. Hank Lim's arguments can be accessed at http://www.siiaonline.org/scm/articles/singapore_perception_of_ajcep.pdf.

15. Ong Keng Yong, Secretary-General of ASEAN, "Integrating Southeast Asian Economies: Challenges for ASEAN" (Remarks at the ASEAN Energy Business Forum 2004, Manila, Philippines, 8 June 2004).
16. Lim, op. cit.

9

ASEAN–Korea Co-operation in the Development of New ASEAN Members: Korea's ODA Policy

Sung-Hoon Park

INTRODUCTION

Korea was one of the major beneficiaries of international aid activities from the 1960s to the 1980s. Korea quickly reconstructed itself after the Korean War of 1950–53 and soon emerged as one of the world's leading manufacturers of selected industrial products, such as home electronics, ships, and cars. Little wonder then that a number of international development organizations (including the World Bank) termed Korea's economic development over the last five decades a "miracle".[1] However, it should be noted that Korea had benefited substantially from assistance provided by the international community. The international aid nurtured Korea's industrial and developmental capacity in three ways. First, during the first decade of the post-Korean War period, the United States provided a total of US$2.5 billion as grant-type aid to Korea. This accounted for about 80 per cent of Korea's total fixed capital formation.[2] The total amount of Official Development Assistance (ODA) received by Korea in the years 1945–80 is reported to be US$20.3 billion. This sum can be subdivided into grants of US$4.5 billion and loans of US$15.8 billion.

Second, numerous developed countries had provided Korea with technical assistance, thereby aiding in the development of its industrial capacity and market economy system. Third, Korea is a long-time developing country, and due to its status as such, it was granted preferential access when it exported to its major trading partners. This was especially so under the generalized system of preferences (GSP) scheme, which lasted until the mid-1990s.

Since becoming a newly industrialized economy (NIE) in the mid-1980s, Korea has begun to provide ODA. The establishment of the Economic Development and Co-operation Fund (EDCF) in 1987 under the auspices of the Korea Eximbank marked the beginning of Korean activity in dispensing ODA. The EDCF provided developing countries with loans for the development of their industrial capacity, the stabilization of their economies, and to strengthen their economic ties with Korea. Following the EDCF, the Korean Government established the Korea International Co-operation Agency (KOICA), which has since been responsible for grant-type aid. The development assistance programmes of Korea have been largely managed by these two institutions. Given that East Asia is Korea's largest trading partner, much of Korea's ODA is centred in this region.

This chapter seeks to provide an overview of Korea's ODA policy towards East Asian developing countries, specifically Cambodia, Laos, Myanmar, and Vietnam (CLMV). In so doing, the desirability and future direction of this policy will be discussed. Section two of this chapter discusses the main features of Korea's overall ODA policy. Section three analyses Korea's overall ODA policy by comparing it to selected member countries of the Organization for Economic Co-operation and Development's (OECD) Development Assistance Committee (DAC). Section four looks into Korea's ODA activities *vis-à-vis* CLMV, which is followed by the conclusion in section five.

CHANGES IN INTERNATIONAL ENVIRONMENT OF DEVELOPMENT ASSISTANCE AND KOREA

The Millennium Development Goals (MDGs), adopted by the United Nations General Assembly in 2000, is the most important framework for the current international development assistance activities. The MDGs' eight most immediate goals seek to reduce alienation and poverty prevailing in the developing and least-developed countries: (1) eradicate extreme poverty and hunger; (2) ensure universal primary education; (3) promote gender equality and empower women; (4) reduce child mortality; (5) improve internal health; (6) combat HIV/AIDS, malaria, and other diseases; (7) ensure environmental sustainability; and (8) develop a global partnership for development. It is often suggested that the MDGs have set a new direction for international co-operation in the twenty-first century, with its strong emphasis on the global dimension of poverty and hunger. Indeed, poverty and hunger are no longer merely the problems of developing countries. Accordingly, the MDGs have declared that partnership between developing and developed countries is the main guiding principle for the international community's future development assistance activities.[3]

Since adopting the so-called Paris Declaration in March 2005, DAC has developed a twelve-point Indicators of Progress, which is used to evaluate the effectiveness of development assistance programmes. These indicators include twelve check points grouped into four broader categories: (1) Ownership of recipients; (2) Alignment; (3) Harmonization; and (4) Management for results.[4] By extension, the importance of making the development assistance increasingly "untied" with the procurement of products originating from donor countries is also highlighted.[5]

As Korea is faced with these changes in the international environment of development assistance activities, it is pressed to improve its development assistance policy. A thorough review of the national policy of providing development assistance was conducted by the Ministry of Foreign Affairs and Trade (MOFAT) and KOICA in 2005. It revealed the following deficiencies: (1) insufficient amount of ODA *vis-à-vis* the country's GDP and international role; (2) the ODA is unevenly distributed; (3) recipient countries receive relatively low amounts of ODA; (4) lack of specialized human resources; (5) insufficient consideration of recipients' needs; (6) relatively low participation of non-governmental sectors; (7) non-existence of strategic focus and result-oriented projects, etc. Thus, as an OECD member country with hopes of joining DAC in the near future, Korea is facing enormous challenges.

MAIN FEATURES OF KOREA'S OVERALL ODA POLICY

Trends in Korea's ODA Activities

Recent statistics reveal that Korea's ODA, which stood at approximately US$111 million in 1993, has increased substantially over the past few years, reaching US$400 million in 2004 (see Table 9.1). The fourfold increase in the absolute amount of ODA within this reported eleven-year period is remarkable, given the country's short period as an ODA donor.

Table 9.1
Overview of Korea's ODA, 1993–2004
(US$ million)

	1993	1994	1995	1996	1997	1998	1999	2000	2001	2002	2003	2004*
ODA	111.56	140.22	115.99	159.15	185.61	182.71	317.49	212.07	264.65	278.78	365.91	403.25
Bilateral aid	60.12	60.07	71.46	123.31	111.34	124.70	131.35	131.19	171.54	206.76	245.17	311.63
Grants	32.68	38.45	50.11	53.41	54.77	37.21	38.95	47.78	52.97	66.70	145.46	192.95
Loans	27.44	21.62	21.35	69.90	56.57	87.49	92.40	83.41	118.57	140.06	99.71	118.68
Multilateral aid	51.44	80.15	44.53	35.84	74.27	58.01	186.14	80.88	93.11	72.02	120.74	91.62
Grants to international organizations	10.25	12.88	14.82	30.08	29.06	33.59	67.70	25.27	60.10	50.69	84.92	n.a.
Capital subscriptions to international organizations	25.67	25.65	22.68	5.76	35.53	28.32	129.46	68.34	35.03	34.45	52.53	n.a.
Other aid	15.52	41.62	7.03	–	9.68	–3.90	–11.02	–12.73	–2.03	–13.14	–16.72	n.a.
GNI (US$100 million)	3,308	3,780	4,526	4,804	4,374	3,168	4,021	4,552	4,213	4,770	5,761	6,809
ODA/GNI (%)	0.034	0.037	0.026	0.033	0.042	0.058	0.079	0.047	0.063	0.058	0.064	0.059

*Figures for 2004 are provisional.
Source: KOICA, internal documents.

Korea's ODA policy favours bilateral aid to multilateral one. Its bilateral ODA traditionally focuses on loan-type assistance rather than grant-type assistance. However, this focus has recently shifted to the grant-type assistance. For the first time in its recent history, grant-type assistance exceeded the loan-type assistance in 2003. This shift to dispensing grant-type assistance was maintained in 2004.

Despite this, Korea lags behind the other OECD member countries in DAC in terms of ODA *vis-à-vis* the country's gross national income (GNI). Whereas the ODA/GNI ratios of more than half of the DAC member countries (twelve of twenty-two) exceed 0.3 per cent, it is only 0.06 per cent for Korea. The average DAC member countries' ODA/GNI ratio was approximately 0.25 per cent in 2004, with five countries — Norway (0.87 per cent), Luxembourg (0.85 per cent), Denmark (0.84 per cent), Sweden (0.77 per cent), and the Netherlands (0.74 per cent) — fulfilling the non-binding recommendation of DAC to provide more than 0.7 per cent of GNI as ODA (see Table 9.2).

In 2003 Korea directed more than 60 per cent of its bilateral aid to Asia (61.3 per cent), 17.2 per cent to the Middle East, and 7.7 per cent to Africa. Of the US$150 million provided to Asian developing countries, 44 per cent were in grants, and the remaining 56 per cent were in the form of loans (see Table 9.3). This strong focus on Asia is in line with the trade and investment orientation of Korean firms. The ODA therefore functions as a complementary instrument in strengthening economic ties with Asian countries.

Korea's ODA Policy in International Comparison

A low ODA/GNI ratio is a characteristic of Korea's current ODA policy. The Korean Government has been making efforts to increase this ratio ever since the country's accession to the OECD in 1996. However, there has not been any substantial progress. A recent speech given by the KOICA president reveals that the government intends to increase this ratio at least to 0.1 per cent by 2009.[6] When compared to the average ratio of 0.25 per cent of DAC member countries, this is still well below international standards.

In the composition of bilateral ODA and specifically in the share of the grant element in total bilateral ODA, Korea lags far behind the great majority of DAC member countries. Table 9.4 shows that the share of the "grant element"[7] in Korea's bilateral ODA is a mere 61.9 per cent, whereas the same ratios of all the DAC member countries except Spain (81.9 per cent) and Portugal (20.3 per cent) are higher than 95 per cent. With the debt relief for least-developed countries taken into account additionally, a number of DAC member countries recorded the grant element higher than 100 per cent.

Table 9.2
ODA/GNI Ratios in International Comparison, 2001–04
(US$ million)

Country	2004*		2003		2002		2001	
	ODA	ODA/GNI (%)	ODA	ODA/GNI (%)	ODA	ODA/GNI (%)	ODA	ODA/GNI (%)
Australia	1,465	0.25	1,219	0.25	989	0.26	873	0.25
Austria	691	0.24	505	0.20	520	0.26	533	0.29
Belgium	1,452	0.41	1,853	0.60	1,072	0.43	867	0.37
Canada	2,537	0.26	2,031	0.24	2,004	0.28	1,533	0.22
Denmark	2,025	0.84	1,748	0.84	1,643	0.96	1,634	1.03
Finland	655	0.35	558	0.35	462	0.35	389	0.32
France	8,475	0.42	7,253	0.41	5,486	0.38	4,198	0.32
Germany	7,497	0.28	6,784	0.28	5,324	0.27	4,990	0.27
Greece	464	0.23	362	0.21	276	0.21	202	0.17
Ireland	586	0.39	504	0.39	398	0.40	287	0.33
Italy	2,484	0.15	2,433	0.17	2,332	0.20	1,627	0.15
Japan	8,859	0.19	8,880	0.20	9,283	0.23	9,847	0.23
Luxembourg	241	0.85	194	0.81	147	0.77	139	0.76
Netherlands	4,235	0.74	3,981	0.80	3,338	0.81	3,172	0.82
New Zealand	210	0.23	165	0.23	122	0.22	112	0.25

Table 9.2 (continued)

Country	2004*		2003		2002		2001	
	ODA	ODA/GNI (%)	ODA	ODA/GNI (%)	ODA	ODA/GNI (%)	ODA	ODA/GNI (%)
Norway	2,200	0.87	2,042	0.92	1.696	0.89	1,346	0.80
Portugal	1,028	0.63	320	0.22	323	0.27	268	0.25
Spain	2,547	0.26	1,961	0.23	1,712	0.26	1,737	0.30
Sweden	2,704	0.77	2,400	0.79	2,012	0.84	1,666	0.77
Switzerland	1,379	0.37	1,299	0.39	939	0.32	908	0.34
United Kingdom	7,836	0.36	6,282	0.34	4,924	0.31	4,579	0.32
United States	18,999	0.16	16,254	0.15	13,290	0.13	11,429	0.11
Total	78,568	0.25	69,029	0.25	58,292	0.23	52,335	0.22
Korea	403	0.06	366	0.06	279	0.06	265	0.06

*Figures for 2004 are provisional.
Source: KOICA, internal documents.

Table 9.3
Geographical Distribution of Korean ODA, 2003
(US$ million)

	Grants			Loans			Total	%
	Amount	%	No. of Nations	Amount	%	No. of Nations		
Europe	0.89	0.6	6	2.17	2.2	2	3.06	1.2
Africa	8.96	6.2	40	10.02	10.0	3	18.98	7.7
Latin America	7.23	5.0	30	3.93	3.9	3	11.16	4.6
Asia	66.01	45.4	26	84.28	84.5	11	150.29	61.3
Middle East	42.39	29.1	10	-0.22	-0.2	1	42.17	17.2
Oceania	5.31	3.7	8	-0.47	-0.5	1	4.84	2.0
Others	14.66	10.1	–	0.00	0.0	–	14.66	6.0
Subtotal	145.45	100.0	120	99.71	100.0	21	245.16	100.0
United Nations	25.10		–	–		–	25.10	20.8
World Bank	52.53		–	–		–	52.53	43.5
RDA[1]	34.29		–	–		–	34.29	28.4
Miscellaneous	25.53		–	-16.72		–	8.81	7.3
Subtotal	137.46		–	-16.72		–	120.74	100.0
Total	282.91		120	82.99		21	365.9	–
Bilateral	4.34		17	-1.25		2	3.09	
Multilateral	3.56		–	0		–	3.56	
Total	7.90		17	-1.25		2	6.65	
Grand total	290.81		137	81.74		23	372.55	

Row groupings (left margin): Bilateral Aid / Multilateral Aid = ODA; OA[2]

Notes: [1]RDA—Regional development agency.
[2]Aid for the nations which are under Part II (former Soviet Union and developing countries) is distinguished as OA (official aid) rather than ODA, according to the categorization breakdown of countries in OECD/DAC.
Source: KOICA, internal documents.

Table 9.4
Composition of Bilateral ODA in International Comparison, 2004
(US$ million)

Country	Bilateral ODA	Grants	Loans	Share of Grants (%)
Australia	1,193	1,193	–	100.0
Austria	366	369	–4	101.0
Belgium	873	924	–51	105.9
Canada	1,839	1,870	–31	101.7
Denmark	1,190	1,195	–5	100.4
Finland	362	353	9	97.6
France	5,764	6,094	–329	105.7
Germany	3,939	4,582	–643	116.3
Greece	352	352	–	100.0
Ireland	410	410	–	100.0
Italy	741	894	–153	120.6
Japan	5,871	7,120	–1,250	121.3
Luxembourg	164	164	–	100.0
Netherlands	3,038	3,607	–569	118.7
New Zealand	159	159	–	100.0
Norway	1,537	1,496	41	97.3
Portugal	871	177	694	20.3
Spain	1,449	1,186	263	81.9
Sweden	2,047	2,037	10	99.5
Switzerland	1,022	1,008	14	98.6
United Kingdom	5,283	5,039	244	95.4
United States	15,012	15,805	–792	105.3
Total	53,480	56,034	–2,554	104.8
Korea	311.6	193	119	61.9

Note: Figures for 2004 are provisional.
Source: KOICA, internal documents.

Similarly, Korea lags behind in per-capita ODA. While Table 9.5 illustrates that Korea's per-capita ODA has increased substantially over the last decade, its level of average per-capita ODA is one-tenth that of the DAC member countries. Norway and Luxembourg have been at the top of the list with fifty times higher ODA per capita than Korea.

The share of tied aid is another part of Korea's ODA that has to be analysed. Whereas the share of tied aid of the great majority of DAC member countries is kept below 20 per cent, and their average ratio is below 7 per cent, more than 95 per cent of Korea's ODA is either partially tied (16.9 per cent) or fully tied (80.6 per cent) (see Table 9.6). It is generally understood that

Table 9.5
Per-capita ODA in International Comparison

Country	Per-capita ODA (US$)		Assistance through NGOs	
	1992–93	2002–03	Amount (2003) (US$ million)	ODA/GNI (2002–03) (%)
Australia	52	50	337	0.07
Austria	23	58	71	0.03
Belgium	76	125	165	0.04
Canada	79	59	566	0.05
Denmark	249	285	–	–
Finland	94	89	13	0.01
France	126	96	–	–
Germany	79	66	1,008	0.04
Greece	–	26	8	0.00
Ireland	24	103	283	0.16
Italy	57	37	27	0.00
Japan	79	69	335	0.01
Luxembourg	109	344	7	0.02
Netherlands	170	203	300	0.06
New Zealand	28	32	18	0.03
Norway	302	381	–	0.11
Portugal	27	28	4	0.00
Spain	33	39	–	–
Sweden	195	221	23	0.01
Switzerland	140	141	280	0.08
United Kingdom	62	89	389	0.02
United States	51	51	6,326	0.06
Total	72	69	10,162	0.04
Korea	2.1	7	59	–

Source: KOICA, internal documents.

the higher the share of untied aid, the higher the odds that the aid is used for humanitarian purposes. Therefore, a high share of tied loans strongly suggests that Korea's ODA funds are still used primarily for commercial purposes.

POSITION OF CLMV IN KOREA'S ODA STATISTICS

Overall Feature

Table 9.7 shows a list of the twenty top recipients of Korea's ODA in 2003. Iraq, Indonesia, and Afghanistan were the three largest recipients of Korea's ODA funds in that year. This was in response to the 11 September 2001 terrorist attacks and the U.S. war against terror. Iraq and Afghanistan were devastated by the U.S. war against terror, and Indonesia was hit by several terrorist attacks during 2003, thereby motivating the international community to help them rebuild democracy and their economies. Korea was no exception to this trend.

It is quite encouraging to find all CLMV countries on the list of the twenty largest recipients of Korea's ODA, with Vietnam, Cambodia, Myanmar, and Laos ranking sixth, eighth, tenth, and seventeenth respectively. However, many indicators suggest that Korea's ODA has minimal impact on the economic and social development of the recipients.

Table 9.6
Share of Tied Loans in International Comparison, 2003
(In percentages)

Country	Untied	Partially Tied	Tied
Australia	67.2	–	32.8
Austria	51.4	–	48.6
Belgium	99.1	–	0.9
Canada	52.6	0.0	47.4
Denmark	71.5	–	28.5
Finland	85.8	–	14.2
France	93.1	3.9	3.1
Germany	94.6	–	5.4
Greece	93.8	1.2	5.0
Ireland	100.0	–	–
Italy	Not Reported	Not Reported	Not Reported
Japan	96.1	0.5	3.4
Luxembourg	Not Reported	Not Reported	Not Reported
Netherlands	Not Reported	Not Reported	Not Reported
New Zealand	81.4	–	18.6
Norway	99.9	–	0.1
Portugal	93.7	–	6.3
Spain	55.8	0.2	44.0
Sweden	93.6	6.4	–
Switzerland	96.4	–	3.6
United Kingdom	100.0	–	–
United States	Not Reported	Not Reported	Not Reported
Total	92.0	1.2	6.8
Korea	2.5	16.9	80.6

Note: Technical co-operation and administrative costs are excluded.
Source: KOICA, internal documents.

Table 9.7
Top Twenty Korean ODA Recipient Countries in 2003
(US$ million)

Rank	Country	Amount	Percentage
1	Iraq	40.57	16.5
2	Indonesia	30.17	12.3
3	Afghanistan	21.12	8.6
4	Sri Lanka	17.15	7.0
5	China	16.40	6.7
6	Vietnam	12.68	5.2
7	Ghana	12.38	5.0
8	Cambodia	10.76	4.4
9	Bangladesh	10.07	4.1
10	Myanmar	6.64	2.7
Subtotal for top 10	–	177.94	72.6
11	Philippines	6.04	2.5
12	Mongolia	5.91	2.4
13	Nicaragua	4.26	1.7
14	Croatia	2.83	1.2
15	Micronesia	2.57	1.0
16	Kazakhstan	2.42	1.0
17	Laos	2.11	0.9
18	Peru	2.09	0.9
19	Thailand	1.72	0.7
20	Egypt	1.71	0.7
Subtotal for top 20	–	209.60	85.5
Grand total	–	245.16	100.0

Source: KOICA, internal documents.

Korean developmental aid to CLMV tends to be concentrated on four main fields of activities: development study, social and economic infrastructure projects, dispatching of volunteers, and training of industrial workers. In contrast, other aid activities, such as inviting experts, dispatching of medical doctors and Taekwondo teachers, and emergency relief, have not been extensively utilized by Korea's development co-operation agencies. The following sub-section provides more country-specific analyses of the current bilateral ODA situation.

Country-Specific Features

Cambodia

Cambodia has become one of Korea's key focal points in its recent ODA policy. For the last four years, the annual ODA to Cambodia has more than trebled, reaching US$3.3 million in 2004. The total bilateral aid to Cambodia during the period 2001–04 stood at US$8.5 million (see Table 9.8).

Unlike the other countries, Korean ODA to Cambodia is relatively evenly distributed among the three core areas of development co-operation: development study (27 per cent of total ODA allocated during 2001–04), social and economic infrastructure projects (26 per cent), and training of industrial workers (23 per cent). During 2001–04, a total of 480 industrial workers were invited to Korea and trained, and approximately fifty volunteers were sent to ensure that the country was able to cope with the basic needs, and develop industrial and other capacities. Korea's involvement in areas of development assistance, such as social and economic infrastructure projects, and sending volunteers, Taekwondo trainers and co-operation agents, is a recent phenomenon. The reason for this lies in Cambodia's present political and social stability.

Since the accession of Cambodia into the World Trade Organization (WTO), KOICA has launched another US$1 million project, aimed at improving the country's capacity in conducting its trade policy in line with the WTO rules. The Korea Institute for International Economic Policy (KIEP) was commissioned to execute this project, which lapsed at the beginning of 2006.

Laos

Laos is the seventeenth largest recipient of Korean ODA, with the share of 0.9 per cent. Nevertheless, the ODA amount of the last four years has recorded a nearly 500 per cent increase, surpassing the speed of increase registered for all the other three countries in CLMV (see Table 9.9).

Unlike Cambodia, Korean ODA to Laos is more unevenly distributed, with the social and economic infrastructure projects assuming more than 40 per cent of total ODA amount provided during 2001–04, followed by dispatching volunteers (21 per cent), and training of industrial workers (16 per cent). Over the reported four-year period, a total of 284 industrial workers were invited for training purposes, and 66 volunteers were dispatched. In contrast to the other countries in the CLMV group, the provision of materials and facilities uses a relatively high portion of the ODA.

Myanmar

Korea's ODA to Myanmar, like that to Cambodia and Laos, has increased substantially over the last four years. This reflects a strengthened aid activity of Korea towards East Asian developing countries in the twenty-first century (see Table 9.10).

Table 9.8
Korea's Bilateral ODA to Cambodia, 2001–04

Projects	Unit	2001	2002	2003	2004	Total
Total amount	US$1,000	1,056.06	1,764.85	2,340.72	3,340.97	8,502.60
Invitation of trainees	US$1,000	366.09	589.94	534.68	437.38	1,928.08
	Number	112 (112)	128 (128)	136 (136)	108 (108)	484 (484)
Invitation of experts	US$1,000	35.14	52.61	39.6	152.76	280.11
	Number	3 (3)	2 (2)	2 (2)	3 (3)	10 (10)
Medical doctors	US$1,000	46.12	115.02	121.71	145.41	428.25
	Number	1 (1)	1 (0)	1 (0)	1 (0)	4 (1)
Taekwondo teachers	US$1,000	49.49	59.51	69.26	95	273.27
	Number	1 (0)	1 (0)	1 (0)	1 (0)	4 (0)
Volunteers	US$1,000	0	0	24.79	678.34	703.13
	Number	0 (0)	0 (0)	4 (4)	43 (39)	47 (43)
Co-operation agents	US$1,000	0	0	3.3	28.21	31.51
	Number	0 (0)	0 (0)	1 (1)	2 (1)	3 (2)
Development study	US$1,000	429.55	228.36	960.91	686.21	2,305.04
	Number	1 (1)	2 (1)	2 (1)	3 (1)	8 (4)
Materials, facilities	US$1,000	129.66	181.84	66.32	0	377.83
	Number	3 (3)	3 (3)	3 (3)	0 (0)	9 (9)
Infrastructure projects	US$1,000	0	537.58	520.15	1,117.65	2,175.38
	Number	0 (0)	1 (1)	1 (0)	2 (1)	4 (2)

Source: KOICA, internal documents.

Table 9.9
Korea's Bilateral ODA to Laos, 2001–04

Projects	Units	2001	2002	2003	2004	Total
Total amount	US$1,000	680.4	1,418.99	2,028.35	3,378.88	7,506.62
Invitation of trainees	US$1,000	189.7	436	297.38	277.31	1,200.39
	Number	59 (59)	92 (92)	75 (75)	58 (58)	284 (284)
Invitation of experts	US$1,000	0.53	0	29.1	109.03	138.67
	Number	1 (0)	0 (0)	1 (1)	1 (1)	3 (2)
Medical doctors	US$1,000	58.15	0	0	0	58.15
	Number	1 (0)	0 (0)	0 (0)	0 (0)	1 (0)
Volunteers	US$1,000	137.14	193.34	329.06	920.78	1,580.31
	Number	7 (4)	11 (4)	14 (7)	34 (23)	66 (38)
Co-operation agents	US$1,000	8.1	65.15	94.63	113.82	281.69
	Number	4 (4)	7 (3)	11 (4)	14 (4)	36 (15)
Co-operation doctors	US$1,000	0	0	53.73	68.01	121.74
	Number	0 (0)	0 (0)	1 (1)	1 (0)	2 (1)
Materials, facilities	US$1,000	66.99	232.81	49.98	407.34	757.11
	Number	2 (2)	3 (3)	1 (1)	1 (1)	7 (7)
Emergency relief	US$1,000	10.2	0	0	0	10.2
	Number	1 (1)	0 (0)	0 (0)	0 (0)	1 (1)
Infrastructure projects	US$1,000	175.35	450.68	1,122.39	1,435.72	3,184.15
	Number	1 (1)	2 (1)	3 (0)	2 (1)	8 (3)
Assistance to NGOs	US$1,000	34.24	41.02	52.08	46.88	174.21
	Number	1 (1)	1 (1)	1 (1)	1 (1)	4 (4)

Source: KOICA, internal documents.

Table 9.10
Korea's Bilateral ODA to Myanmar, 2001–04

Projects	Units	2001	2002	2003	2004	Total
Total amount	US$1,000	651.2	1,574.40	1,460.42	2,045.07	5,731.08
Invitation of trainees	US$1,000	222.97	564.2	409.52	336.65	1,533.35
	Number	64 (64)	106 (106)	96 (96)	74 (74)	340 (340)
Invitation of experts	US$1,000	69.19	42.43	21.63	37.43	170.69
	Number	3 (3)	2 (2)	1 (1)	1 (1)	7 (7)
Medical doctors	US$1,000	44.58	111.32	107.4	129.49	392.78
	Number	1 (1)	1 (0)	1 (0)	1 (0)	4 (1)
Taekwondo teachers	US$1,000	75.98	83.14	1.83	47.33	208.28
	Number	1 (0)	1 (0)	0 (0)	1 (1)	3 (1)
Volunteers	US$1,000	61.4	259.8	295.33	339.96	956.49
	Number	11 (7)	15 (6)	14 (2)	23 (17)	63 (32)
Co-operation agents	US$1,000	5.26	35.82	59.37	101.26	201.71
	Number	2 (2)	4 (2)	8 (4)	10 (2)	24 (10)
Development study	US$1,000	171.82	297.81	520.35	235.59	1,225.57
	Number	1 (1)	2 (1)	2 (1)	3 (0)	8 (3)
Materials, facilities	US$1,000	0	151.16	7.79	20.43	179.38
	Number	0 (0)	1 (1)	1 (1)	1 (1)	3 (3)
Infrastructure projects	US$1,000	0	0	6.81	769.36	776.18
	Number	0 (0)	0 (0)	0 (0)	2 (2)	2 (2)
Assistance to NGOs	US$1,000	0	28.71	30.38	27.57	86.66
	Number	0 (0)	1 (1)	1 (1)	1 (1)	3 (3)

Source: KOICA, internal documents.

The three main areas into which Korean ODA funds are channelled are: the invitation of industrial workers for training purposes (27 per cent), the conducting of development studies (21 per cent), and the dispatching of volunteers (17 per cent), followed by the construction of economic and social infrastructure projects (14 per cent). Over the reported four-year period, a total of 340 industrial workers were invited for training, and sixty-three volunteer workers and twenty-four co-operation agents were dispatched to Myanmar. A sum of nearly US$87,000 was provided to Myanmar through local non-governmental organizations (NGOs).

Vietnam

Vietnam has been the largest recipient of Korean ODA funds in the CLMV group. Its total ODA in 2001–04 amounted to US$23 million, as shown in Table 9.11.

The construction of economic and social infrastructure projects, training of industrial workers, and supporting volunteer activities constituted three areas in which Korean ODA was used in Vietnam. In addition, a number of development studies have been conducted through bilateral development assistance.

EVALUATION AND POLICY RECOMMENDATIONS

This chapter comparatively analysed Korea's overall ODA policy, and briefly discussed the main uses of Korean ODA in CLMV. Due to restrictions of data on ODA for certain countries, a detailed analysis could not yet be provided. The discussion thus far, however, reveals a number of tasks the Korean ODA policy has to tackle in the medium and long term.

First, it is of utmost importance that Korea joins DAC in the near future. Korea has already been granted observer status upon its accession to the OECD in 1996. Given that all the twenty-two developed countries in the OECD are members of DAC, and the fact that the most recent membership expansion dates back to 1991 when Spain, Portugal, and Greece joined DAC, Korea is desirous of joining the bandwagon. In a recent KOICA-funded seminar, Chang (2005*a*) recommended that the Korean Government carefully stage its accession strategy to DAC, suggesting that 2008 should be its target year of accession. He recommended that the government declare its readiness to accede to DAC in 2006, as it marks Korea's tenth year as an official member of the OECD.

Table 9.11
Korea's Bilateral ODA to Vietnam, 2001–04

Projects	Units	2001	2002	2003	2004	Total
Total amount	US$1,000	4,814.11	4,705.65	3,514.60	9,789.17	22,823.54
Invitation of trainees	US$1,000	758.32	846.39	713.41	730.28	3,048.40
	Number	221 (221)	227 (227)	175 (175)	180 (180)	803 (803)
Invitation of experts	US$1,000	75.85	50.24	37.82	45.8	209.71
	Number	3 (2)	2 (2)	3 (3)	4 (4)	12 (11)
Medical doctors	US$1,000	0	0	0	104.76	104.76
	Number	0 (0)	0 (0)	0 (0)	1 (1)	1 (1)
Taekwondo teachers	US$1,000	44.15	55.64	58.4	72.25	230.44
	Number	1 (0)	1 (0)	1 (0)	1 (0)	4 (0)
Volunteers	US$1,000	292.49	439.02	490.49	1,339.41	2,561.41
	Number	21 (10)	27 (11)	26 (6)	64 (50)	138 (77)
Co-operation agents	US$1,000	124.75	76.11	118.36	188.46	507.69
	Number	8 (0)	10 (5)	9 (4)	16 (7)	43 (16)
Co-operation doctors	US$1,000	87.67	53.25	80.85	26.56	248.33
	Number	2 (1)	2 (0)	1 (0)	1 (0)	6 (1)
Development study	US$1,000	546.11	580.33	15.09	95.04	1,236.57
	Number	3 (1)	2 (1)	1 (0)	1 (0)	7 (2)

Table 9.11 *(continued)*

Projects	Units	2001	2002	2003	2004	Total
Materials, facilities	US$1,000	0	129.78	0	0	129.78
	Number	0 (0)	2 (2)	0 (0)	0 (0)	2 (2)
Emergency relief	US$1,000	0	10.13	10.14	30.27	50.54
	Number	0 (0)	1 (1)	1 (1)	1 (1)	3 (3)
Infrastructure projects	US$1,000	2,776.47	2,393.39	1,911.04	7,035.94	14,116.85
	Number	7 (5)	6 (1)	3 (1)	5 (3)	21 (10)
Assistance to NGOs	US$1,000	108.3	71.37	78.98	120.41	379.06
	Number	4 (4)	3 (3)	4 (4)	4 (4)	15 (15)

Source: KOICA, internal documents.

Second, in order to acquire the DAC membership the Korean Government has to make every effort to upgrade its ODA policy. As the analyses in section two revealed, Korea is lagging far behind its OECD/DAC fellow countries in all ODA indicators. Having reached the status of a NIE with the aid activities of the international community during the 1950s and 1960s, Korea has to fulfil its responsibility to help the underdeveloped countries upgrade their societies and economies by granting ODA funds conducive to their level of economic development. Korea should raise its ODA/GNI ratio at least up to the level of Italy, which has the lowest ODA/GNI ratio of 0.15 per cent. In this respect, the declared goal of Korea's influential aid institution to increase the ratio to 0.1 per cent by 2009 is an encouraging signal. In fact, the prospective membership of Korea to the OECD/DAC is expected to exercise a needed international peer pressure on Korea's ODA policy. Also, increasing the ODA/GNI ratio will lead to the upgrading of a number of other indicators, including the per-capita ODA.

Third, it is imperative that Korea increases the portions of grant element and untied aid in its overall ODA strategy. Korea has been one of the major beneficiaries of international ODA activities, especially during the first phase of the country's economic development. Reciprocating this aid with increased share of the grant element and untied loans will not only exercise a stronger impact in helping developing countries upgrade their societies and economies, but also improve Korea's profile as well.

Fourth, as the three aforementioned measures will benefit the ASEAN countries, especially CLMV, Korea should strengthen its efforts to share the country's development experiences with these countries. Korea could increase the ODA elements such as training of industrial workers, conducting of development studies, and invitation and training of experts, thereby contributing to the expansion of its counterparts' development, human resource capacities, and their sustainable development. This policy reorientation is expected to help CLMV more strongly than other developing countries, because they possess a number of preconditions for successful development strategies. A recent policy initiative of Korea also acknowledges the importance of focusing on its core competence area, namely human resources development.[8]

Although it is not directly related to ODA policy, a provision of preferential market access, through the GSP, for strategic products of CLMV is desirable for CLMV to improve their industrialization strategies. Labour-intensive products, such as textiles and apparel, standardized consumer electronics, and footwear, are ideal for an effective GSP scheme. As it is permitted for importing countries to exercise a certain degree of discretion when designing the GSP scheme, Korea can assemble a more comprehensive and far-reaching GSP scheme specifically for CLMV than is currently provided to other countries.

NOTES

*The author appreciates the research assistance provided by Yoongu Chung.
1. See, for example, World Bank (1993).
2. Mason et al. (1980).
3. See Chang (2005*b*), pp. 3–5.
4. For details, see OECD (2005).
5. Ibid.
6. See Kim (2005).
7. The grant element is calculated by (nominal value of ODA — Net Present Value of ODA [10 per cent discount]) divided by the nominal value of ODA. The grant element must exceed 25 per cent. This is one of three main conditions set by DAC.
8. See MOFAT and KOICA (2005).

REFERENCES

Chang, Hyunsik. "Evaluation of Korea's Membership to the Development Assistance Committee (DAC) of OECD". In *Future Direction of Korea's ODA Policy*. Seoul: KOICA, 2005*a*. Proceeding of the seminar hosted by KOICA and Ewha Women's University on 28 June 2005.

———. "Changes in International Environments Surrounding ODA and Korea's Response". Mimeographed. 2005*b*.

Kim, Seok-Hyun. "Opening Speech". In *Future Direction of Korea's ODA Policy*. Seoul: KOICA, 2005. Proceeding of the seminar hosted by KOICA and Ewha Women's University on 28 June 2005.

Mason, E. et al. *The Economic and Social Modernization of the Republic of Korea*. Cambridge, Mass.: Harvard University Press, 1980.

Ministry of Foreign Affairs and Trade (MOFAT) and Korea International Co-operation Agency (KOICA). "Korea's ODA Strategy for 2006–2008: A Draft". Mimeographed. Seoul, 2005.

Organization for Economic Co-operation and Development (OECD). *Paris Declaration on Aid Effectiveness*. Paris: OECD, 2005.

World Bank. *The East Asian Miracle: Economic Growth and Public Policy*. London: Oxford University Press, 1993.

PART V

ASEAN–Korea Co-operation Towards Strengthening East Asian Integration

10

Next Steps in ASEAN–Korea Relations for East Asian Security

Edy Prasetyono

INTRODUCTION

Despite increasing economic interdependence, some formalized free trade agreements, and investments, the security aspects of East Asian co-operation remain uncertain. East Asia is continually beset by tensions arising from the rise of China, Sino–United States rivalry for regional hegemony, the question of Japan's foreign and defence policies, as well as the North Korean nuclear issue. Complicated by territorial conflicts, historical resentment, and domestic dynamics of the countries in the region due to economic and political crises, these developments cast some doubts over the pragmatism of East Asian integration, particularly in the security realm. This chapter attempts to explore whether ASEAN and Korea's contribution to security co-operation is able to strengthen East Asian integration.

SECURITY SITUATION IN EAST ASIA

The most important factor in East Asian security is no doubt the United States. The United States maintains its military alliance with Japan and South Korea. The United States has even appeared to be more comfortable with Japan taking a more active stance in security and foreign security policies, opening the way for a Japanese military role beyond strictly traditional peacekeeping operations. The United States has also expanded military co-operation with non-alliance states, closely co-operated with India to patrol waters approaching the Malacca Straits, and taken some measures to deal with the rapidly increasing influence of China in the region. The United States has taken Proliferation Security Initiatives (PSI) to interdict ships on the high seas suspected of carrying dangerous materials and weapons of mass destruction (WMD) that can be used for terror attacks.

Apart from fighting terrorism and preventing the proliferation of WMD, a more fundamental and long-term strategic interest of the United States in East Asia is to prevent China and Russia from challenging its hegemonic position. No country, other than China and Russia, could potentially challenge the U.S. position in East Asia. Thus, while the United States needs China to counter terrorism and persuade North Korea to return to multilateral talks on the nuclear issue and to readjust to China's growing economy, it continues to try to limit China's influence.

The second factor is Japan. Japan has always been at the centre of strategic calculations in many East Asian states, precisely due to its past behaviour, technological and economic strength for potential military build-up, and political uncertainty in its opening reinterpretation of the Peace Constitution. Moreover, Japan has increased its military operations, developing the missile defence system jointly with the United States. Some observers, particularly in China and Korea, see this as a departure from Japanese traditional stance in defining its international role since the end of World War II. Moreover, Prime Minister Koizumi has been perceived as representing Japanese conservatism in international politics, watching closely China's growing influence in East Asia and Southeast Asia. His visits to the Yasukuni Shrine have poured fuel on the historical hatred and suspicion towards Japan.

Japan–China rivalry is indeed on the rise and perhaps inevitable, resulting in diplomatic offensives towards countries in the region. They compete with each other in having free trade arrangements with ASEAN states, and become more sensitive towards each other over the Taiwan issue, United Nations reform, and arms embargo imposed by the European Union on China.

China is another major factor affecting the security situation in East Asia. Analysis on China's growing economy has led to the conclusion that China will overtake Japan as the world's second largest economy. This has increased China's political and strategic weight, leading to the redistribution of international interests and resources in the region and in the world. China's military build-up is another factor marking China's growing confidence in its diplomatic behaviour, as demonstrated in the case of the Anti-Secessionist

Law (ASL) targeting Taiwan. With interlocking interdependence making military options costlier, it is less likely that China will attack Taiwan under the current international circumstances. The main objective of China's stance towards Taiwan is the prevention of the permanent loss of the renegade province. As a result, China has no compromise policy in opposing "Taiwan independence" secessionist activities, both internally and internationally.

Concerns over China are historically grounded. Any new power coming to the scene has always resulted in a new adjustment of the international system, shaping a new balance of power in global politics. Whether or not China is a threat depends on how the international system creates space for China to get tuned with norms and values the system has developed. But, it also depends on whether China understands its position as a superpower with its responsibility to maintain global stability. A responsible superpower has to make compromises and sacrifices.

Security on the Korean Peninsula is a no less complicated matter. The resumption of the six-party talks looks promising. Japan and North Korea have begun to explore new relations. Social, cultural, and family contacts between the two Koreas have been increasing. However, the political foundation for making sustained peace and enduring stability in the region remains fragile. Domestically, the problems facing the North Korean regime are too complex to be judged purely from the perspective of the nuclear issue. Other issues to consider include the survival of the authoritarian regime, economic failure, and the oppressed population. These factors could in turn shape differences in security interests and, by extension, different means of achieving their security interests. Internationally, East Asia, or Northeast Asia, has failed to develop regional security arrangements, except those anchored under bilateral relations with the United States and those developed and initiated by ASEAN. Lingering problems rooted in territorial disputes and distrust towards each other about their future intentions remain salient factors shaping fragile security in the region.

WHAT CAN ASEAN AND KOREA DO?

Against this backdrop, ASEAN has taken some fundamental measures based on the following suggestions: First, regional stability based on bilateral relations with the United States is inadequate not only due to the nature of new security issues arising from complex interdependence in the political, security, and economic realms that requires multilateral efforts to deal with, but the large U.S. burden as well, for it highlights the uncertainty over the future of U.S. commitment. Leaving this strategic issue unresolved could lead to a vacuum in the strategic thinking of the regional countries, thereby rendering them unprepared to accept any likely reduction of U.S. military presence. This has paved the way for the establishment of the ASEAN Regional Forum (ARF).

Secondly, ASEAN should be more open to political and economic interactions with external powers, and recognize their legitimate interests in the region. This could strike a balance of power or equilibrium in the power structure among major powers outside Southeast Asia.

Thirdly, as China's rise is a reality, ASEAN should engage China. This would lead to more intensive interactions between China and other major powers with ASEAN at the centre.

These calculations reflect ASEAN's position as an independent actor. ASEAN has proven to other countries that it is a benign regional organization without narrow interests and selfishness, and that it is keen on promoting security relations with major external powers. In fact, ASEAN has provided a bridge of interactions for external powers.

Northeast Asia is at the opposite end of the spectrum. The three major Northeast Asian countries are suspicious of each other. The region's lack of definitive regional leadership could be problematic. Japan has economic power, but lacks political leadership; China has strived to expand its political and diplomatic clout in East Asia, but in so doing has proved unacceptable to many neighbouring states. Also, Japan and China are contesting each other for regional hegemony.

It is in this particular context that Korea and ASEAN share a unique and advantageous position. Both can put themselves in a position to lay a bridge for the major powers in East and Southeast Asia. Japan and China cannot do that. Given ASEAN's schemes to bring East Asian countries into closer security interactions, Korea should approach ASEAN so as to fully tap into its unique geopolitical position in Northeast Asia. In so doing, Korea would be able to maintain the balance of power in the region between Japan and China. ASEAN is the ideal mediator for this task as the association has no fear of political, military, and economic threat from Korea. Approaching ASEAN would neutralize China's fear that Korea is acting in the U.S. interests. Likewise, in approaching ASEAN as a mediator, Korea would also be able to show that Japan has no reason to suspect Korean initiatives on regional co-operation, particularly East Asian integration.

Now the question is where Korea and ASEAN should locate themselves in the debate on the East Asia Summit (EAS). The EAS held in Kuala Lumpur in December 2005 was problematic in terms of agenda, membership, and modalities — what makes it different from ASEAN plus Three? When some ASEAN countries demonstrated their reluctant acceptance of the EAS being held in 2005, they feared that the association would be diluted by the big powers in the north, particularly China. With the lack of trust and suspicion towards China's diplomatic offensive, ASEAN and Korea would find that ASEAN plus Three should be the basis for regional integration in East Asia that could be developed in stages comfortable to the member states. The fear of China's diplomatic offensive has been even more valid in the light of the fact that ASEAN has never consolidated its position to pursue an ASEAN Community as outlined in the Bali Concorde II. An EAS could only push some ASEAN member states away from the goal of an ASEAN Community.

ASEAN could ease the U.S. concern over its being marginalized in East Asian dynamics. A China-dominated East Asia would never be acceptable to the United States. The United States is aware that China's assertive diplomacy towards East Asian regionalism is geared towards the reduction of U.S. influence in the region. This would certainly be detrimental to East Asia, as the United States still enjoys a dominant position in strategic and security co-operation in the region. In requesting for ASEAN's presence as a mediator, Korea would be able to prevent Washington from solely relying on Tokyo as its link to East Asian affairs.

CONCLUSION

The opportunities for greater Korean and ASEAN co-operation are many. With great co-operation, Korea could become a leading actor in balancing the volatile relationships of its neighbours in East Asia, thereby assuaging the ASEAN countries' fears of losing their economic interests in the face of Chinese dominance. Given Korea's status as an economic power, its lack of political ambitions, and its situation between Japan and China, mediation from it would be more acceptable to other Asian countries. Co-operation with ASEAN would therefore increase Korea's strategic weight.

As East Asian integration is a long process, the institutional stages and other aspects should be well planned. ASEAN and Korea should learn from the experience of the Asia-Pacific Economic Co-operation (APEC) forum, which is going nowhere. APEC has not proven to be effective in dealing with its member states or actual economic problems. ASEAN should commit more resources if it wishes to be seriously regarded as a regional organization.

REFERENCES

Goh, Evelyn. *Meeting the China Challenge, The US in Southeast Asian Regional Security Strategies*. Washington, D.C.: East-West Center, 2005.

Ho Khai Leong and Samuel Ku, eds. *China and Southeast Asia. Global Changes and Regional Challenges*. Singapore: Institute of Southeast Asian Studies, 2005.

Saw Swee-Hock, Sheng Lijun, and Chin Kin Wah, eds. *ASEAN-China Relations. Realities and Prospects*. Singapore: Institute of Southeast Asian Studies, 2005.

Severino, Rodolfo C. *Towards an ASEAN Security Community*. Singapore: Institute of Southeast Asian Studies, 2004.

Siddique, Sharon and Sree Kumar, compilers. *The 2nd ASEAN Reader*. Singapore: Institute of Southeast Asian Studies, 2003.

11
ASEAN and Korea in East Asian Co-operation

Bae Geung-Chan

RISE OF ASEAN PLUS THREE

In recent years East Asia has been witnessing the emergence of a new regional co-operation framework, namely the Association of Southeast Asian Nations plus Three (ASEAN plus Three). ASEAN plus Three co-operation has indeed gained considerable momentum in a relatively short period without any formal binding agreements among the participating states or a central secretariat. Since the first-ever summit meeting among ASEAN, Korea, China, and Japan in 1997, relations between Southeast Asian and Northeast Asian states have steadily progressed. In the ASEAN plus Three process national leaders as well as finance, economic, and foreign ministers have been meeting regularly. Central bank governors and other senior officials have also begun to hold regular meetings.

In 1998 the East Asia Vision Group (EAVG) was set up to explore ways in which it could expand co-operation in all sectors and at all levels throughout the countries in the region. In 1999 the ASEAN plus Three Summit adopted a Joint Statement on East Asian Co-operation, confirming the political will of East Asian leaders to work towards enhancing intra-regional co-operation. In 2000 the ASEAN plus Three Summit affirmed the Chiang Mai Initiative as one of the most tangible outcomes of ASEAN plus Three co-operation. The Chiang Mai Agreement was to set up a currency swap facility, which would enable the regional countries to respond more effectively to any future financial crisis. The leaders of ASEAN plus Three also agreed to set up the East Asia Study Group (EASG) to implement specific action plans for regional co-operation. In 2001 the ASEAN plus Three Summit reviewed the report of the EAVG, which presented key recommendations for the realization of an East Asian community (EAC). In 2002 the ASEAN plus Three Summit approved the final report of the EASG, including its seventeen short-term measures and nine mid- to long-term measures with high priority, together with its other details.

Another important outcome of the ASEAN plus Three process is the continuation of formal dialogue among the leaders of the Northeast Asian countries of Korea, China, and Japan. On the sidelines of the ASEAN plus Three Summit, the first-ever summit meeting among the leaders of the three countries was held in 1999, thus providing an important milestone for Northeast Asian co-operation as well as East Asian co-operation. Since then, it has been formalized and regularized. In 2001, in order to move towards successful regional integration, the three leaders of Korea, China, and Japan agreed to hold regular foreign affairs and economic ministers meetings and to establish a business forum for Northeast Asia. In 2003 the three Northeast Asian leaders adopted a Joint Declaration on Tripartite Co-operation for the first time in history.

The rise of ASEAN plus Three may be attributed to the launching of the Asia–Europe Meeting (ASEM) in 1996 and the 1997 Asian financial crisis. The European states fostered East Asian co-operation throughout the ASEM process. East Asian countries in particular acutely felt the necessity of regional identity for the first time when they had to negotiate with the highly integrated European Union (EU). In addition, the Asian financial crisis greatly heightened perceptions of economic interdependence between Northeast and Southeast Asia while most extra-regional powers, including the United States and EU, had assumed indifferent attitudes towards the region. At the same time, not only were measures taken by the International Monetary Fund (IMF) largely inappropriate in many cases, the Asia-Pacific Economic Co-operation (APEC), as an Asia-Pacific co-operation mechanism, also did nothing to alleviate the financial crisis. All these factors have given a further boost to the emergence of a sense of community in the region, which awakened the East Asian states to the significance of self-reliant regional co-operation.

OPENING AN EAST ASIA SUMMIT

To date, the most notable outcome of the ASEAN plus Three process is the opening of the East Asia Summit (EAS). In 2004 the leaders of the East Asian states at the Eighth ASEAN plus Three Summit decided to hold the first EAS in December 2005 in Kuala Lumpur, Malaysia.

The idea and concept of an EAS were originally from the two reports of the EAVG and EASG that were led under the initiative of Korea. The main task of the EAVG was to promote the establishment of an EAC. Regarding the establishment of an EAC, one particular recommendation of the EAVG was "the evolution of the annual summit meetings of ASEAN plus Three into the East Asia Summit", which will bring together Korea, China, and Japan on equal terms with Southeast Asian neighbours. Based on the recommendation of the EAVG, the EASG was formed in 2001 to review all EAVG recommendations and to identify all concrete co-operation measures that could help fulfil the vision of an EAC. The EASG report reconfirmed that the EAS was one of the most important medium- and long-term measures, which should be carried out in a step-by-step approach. This was primarily because ASEAN, as a driving force of the ASEAN plus Three process, had expressed some concerns about the possibility that it could be marginalized in a broader context of the EAS.

It should be noted that the EAS as recommended in the EASG report was visualized as a continuation of the ASEAN plus Three process, involving the same thirteen countries and to be held when the ASEAN plus Three process has sufficiently matured. However, such a gradual and incremental approach to the EAS was suddenly abandoned at the Eighth ASEAN plus Three Summit in 2004, so the decision to hold such a summit in 2005 came as a bit of a surprise. In other words, that which was once a mid- to long-term goal had been given a compressed time frame of just one year. More significantly, while previous conventional wisdom was for the ASEAN plus Three Summit to transform itself into an EAS as a move towards an EAC, now the East Asian countries face the prospect of the ASEAN plus Three Summit coexisting with the EAS.

The basic idea was to have the first EAS held back-to-back with the Ninth ASEAN plus Three Summit in Malaysia at the end of 2005. However, several issues still remained, such as establishing a proper relationship between the EAS and the ASEAN plus Three Summit, identifying conceptual differences, determining the frequency and agenda of the EAS, agreeing on future venues, and deciding on participating countries. Among them, the issue of expanding membership has been a key question for both the ASEAN plus Three countries and the countries outside East Asia since it has important implications for the future direction and nature of regional co-operation in the region. It is difficult for any country to deny that East Asian community building should be based on open regionalism. However, if countries such as Australia, New Zealand, India, and the United States are included as member states of the EAS, the differences between the existing APEC and the EAS become rather blurred. More significantly, such inclusions are also likely to bring about fundamental changes in the balance of power among the participant countries of the EAS.

Consequently, ASEAN provided criteria regarding the question of EAS membership at the retreat of ASEAN foreign ministers in April 2005. The criteria set by ASEAN are as follows: first, the new EAS members should be dialogue partners of ASEAN; second, they should maintain substantial co-operative relations with ASEAN; and third, they are signatories to the Treaty of Amity and Co-operation (TAC). According to these criteria, India is already qualified to participate in the EAS and if Australia and New Zealand join TAC, they will be able to participate as well. Since then, New Zealand formally acceded to TAC in July 2005 and Australia demonstrated its intention to accede to TAC in December 2005. ASEAN finally noted that ASEAN, China, Japan, Korea, Australia, India, and New Zealand would participate in the first EAS.

However, Malaysia, as the host country of the EAS, had yet to seek a full consensus among ASEAN members. Up to now, ASEAN countries seem to agree on several points. First, the ASEAN countries should continue to chair the EAS along with the ASEAN plus Three Summit. Second, the EAS will be held once every three years in the capital cities of Southeast Asian countries. Third, the EAS agenda needs to focus on broad political and security issues.

CHINA–JAPAN RIVALRY IN EAST ASIA

Generally speaking, there are several preconditions for successful regional integration, such as a high level of economic interdependence, leadership of hegemonic powers, strong sense of regional identity, external pressure, and so on. Among these, the two most critical conditions are the trade relations between intra-regional states as a demand or economic condition and the existence of a leading power as a supply or political condition.

It is said that East Asia has reasonably sufficient potential for future growth and integration. Although the East Asian economy is still smaller in scale than those of Europe (EU) and North America (North American Free Trade Agreement, NAFTA), what is more important is the fact that its economic growth rate has been much higher than that of any other region. Of course, the East Asian economy suffered a setback due to the 1997 financial crisis, but this has not curtailed its capacity for rapid growth in the future. In addition, the volume of cross-border exchange in East Asia, including Hong Kong and Taiwan, with intra-regional trade accounting for half of overall trade, surpasses that of North America. However, it is considerably lower than that of Europe. Thus it should be noted that East Asia has no less integration potential than North America.

However, the political conditions in East Asia are still uncertain. The stagnating regional integration in East Asia is often ascribed to the absence of leadership despite the presence of the two potential hegemonic powers of China and Japan. On the one hand, Japanese economic dominance in the region is clear given the fact that it accounts for more than 60 per cent of East Asia's GDP and is at least three times larger than the Chinese economy. Besides, Japan is the top aid donor to Southeast Asian countries. On the other hand, the rapid rise of China has become the most critical factor in the international relations of East Asia. China is now the second largest economy in the region. What makes the future strategic picture of the region increasingly complex is the prospect that China will be able to eclipse Japan someday. China is back on the central stage of regional politics with greatly enhanced political and economic clout, and Japan has to find a way to get along with its giant neighbour without losing its power grip in the region.

Despite great progress and promises in China–Japan economic relations, much mutual suspicion remains between the two major powers for historical, territorial, political, military, strategic, and psychological reasons. History has demonstrated that any power transition of this magnitude in international relations tends to be associated with instability and even major power wars. In fact, China has been concerned about the revival of Japanese domination in the region, and Japan has always been worried about China's assertive military practices. It seems quite natural for both China and Japan to see each other as a rival or even as a potential adversary. Therefore, the competition and co-operation between China and Japan will certainly affect every aspect of regional politics in East Asia.

In addition, both major powers have very different interests in regional co-operation and integration. China is more assertive about the idea of Pan-Asian identity and an East Asian bloc. This is in contrast to Japan's broader interests in Asia-Pacific co-operation based on open regionalism. While China envisions itself to be the centre of East Asian regionalism, Japan has by no means accepted this. Particularly, China views the ASEAN plus Three system in which the United States is naturally excluded as a desirable regional grouping needed to hinder the formation of an anti-Chinese alliance network led by the United States. China, as a traditional suzerain power of Asia, also sees ASEAN plus Three as the ideal regional co-operative structure through which to maximize its influence in the region.

As far as ASEAN plus Three co-operation is concerned, the rivalry between these two major powers over the leadership role in East Asia is already on. It was not Japan, but China that took the initiative. At the ASEAN plus Three Summit in 2001, ASEAN and China formally announced their plan to set up a free trade area (FTA) within ten years. While the FTA deal between ASEAN and China would be a new factor to accelerate the formation of an East Asia Free Trade Area (EAFTA) by encouraging other countries, such as Japan and Korea, to facilitate the FTA with ASEAN or formulating an FTA between China, Japan, and Korea, China has some other important political and strategic considerations in mind. China seeks to not only turn ASEAN countries into a pro-China bloc, but also reinforce its connection with the overseas Chinese networks of Southeast Asia in the context of a Greater China.

Alarmed by the initiative taken by China and its continuing diplomatic offensive towards Southeast Asia, Japan feared that ASEAN plus Three may turn into a collective China-led entity against Japan. In the face of the ASEAN–China FTA plan, Japanese responses are basically twofold. One is to strengthen its ties with ASEAN through a massive economic assistance programme, and the other is to conclude FTAs with key countries in the region, as proclaimed by the Koizumi Doctrine. In early 2002 Japan quickly concluded an FTA with Singapore (Japan-Singapore Economic Partnership Agreement or JSEPA), and paved the way to negotiate with Korea on an FTA framework at the governmental level. At the same time, Japan proposed a new EAC, known as the Initiative for Development in East Asia (IDEA), that includes Australia and New Zealand as its core members. The new Japanese version of the EAC not only reflects its broader interest in the Asia-Pacific region, but also its intention to check China's influence in the region.

The second round of Sino–Japanese competition is over the issue of the EAS. Since as early as 2004, China had concentrated its diplomatic efforts on opening the first EAS and hosting the second EAS after Malaysia. At the same time, China demonstrated its strong will to play a leading, if not dominant, role in the process of East Asian community building. China has already presented a series of proposals to kick off the implementation of this process, which included a China-led feasibility study on an EAFTA and, more significantly, hosting a convention of research bodies to draw up plans for regional security integration.

Japan's primary concern with regard to the EAS is simply to contain China. As the issue of the EAS continues to emerge in ASEAN plus Three,

Japan is seeking a way to develop a framework for holding back China, a goal that is very much in line with the United States and part of the alliance relationship. In response, Japan has insisted that the EAS should include the United States and Russia as well as India, Australia, and New Zealand. The primary purpose, of course, is to prevent China from emerging as a dominant power in the process of East Asian regional integration. From Tokyo's point of view, the inclusion of the United States in the EAS is a diluting factor; rather, the U.S. inclusion is preferable to a Beijing-led process of regional integration.

This kind of rivalry is meant to prevent each side from taking on a leadership position in the region. However, both countries are quite reluctant to take a leadership role in the region due to their domestic and external constraints. Japan has not been successful in achieving total regional leadership mainly because of its past history and lack of a sincere apology for its atrocities in World War II. China has unresolved territorial disputes with a number of Southeast Asian countries and its economy is not mature enough to lead regional integration. Put simply, given their present circumstances, neither Japan nor China is to emerge as regional leader. It is also unlikely that China and Japan will play a joint leadership role similar to the French–German dual leadership in the European integration process. The two Asian powers have very different economic and strategic interests that cannot be easily accommodated by political compromises. This is because they are too far apart in many respects to work out a close co-operative relationship.

Nevertheless, it should be stressed that the key to the success of East Asian regional integration lies in the close co-operative relationship between these two major powers. In other words, a joint commitment by China and Japan to East Asian regionalism would greatly enhance the possibility of regional co-operation. But this condition seems very unlikely to be met at the moment.

ROLE OF ASEAN AND KOREA IN EAST ASIAN CO-OPERATION

Who else can play a leading or central role in East Asian co-operation? There are two possible surrogates or substitute powers for a regional leadership position, namely ASEAN and Korea. Although they are not big powers, they possess reasonable potential for leading regional co-operation in East Asia.

ASEAN, as a regional grouping of ten Southeast Asian states, has been playing a pivotal role as a mediator of dialogue between the major powers, including the United States, Japan, and China, in the region. ASEAN has also served as the nucleus of Asia-Pacific co-operation in economic, political, and security matters. ASEAN has created and managed the ASEAN Regional Forum (ARF) process, as the one and only multilateral political and security dialogue mechanism at the governmental level in the Asia-Pacific, since 1994. ASEAN also paved the way for the ASEAN plus Three process as a framework for East Asian co-operation in 1997.

Korea, as a genuine middle power in the region, has been playing an intermediary and conciliatory role. Given Korea's unique geopolitical conditions in Northeast Asia and its location between China and Japan, it could serve as a bridge between the two major powers. Also, in the ASEAN plus Three process, Korea has been playing a co-ordinating role by taking two important initiatives, namely the EAVG and EASG. These two groups have provided the conceptual and methodological foundations for East Asian co-operation.

Certainly, both ASEAN and Korea do not have political, military, and economic capabilities comparable to China and Japan. However, there is relatively more room for the enlargement of the role of ASEAN and Korea since neither of the two big powers is in a good position to lead regional co-operation. That is why ASEAN and Korea need to collaborate with each other on East Asian co-operation as well as in other multilateral forums. In the ASEAN plus Three process, ASEAN and Korea are already playing central roles; ASEAN has provided the hardware, such as the ASEAN plus Three meetings, and Korea has provided the software, such as the EAVG and EASG. Simply put, ASEAN and Korea need to pursue an intra-regional strategic balance by enhancing mutual co-operative relations. Korea's ties with ASEAN, which began in 1989, have greatly expanded with exchanges and co-operation in diverse fields. ASEAN has been a key partner for Korea in discussions on regional and international political matters. It has also become one of Korea's closest economic partners.

We may safely assume that the well-functioning institutional arrangements will greatly contribute to the establishment of a constructive and stable China–Japan relationship as well as the advancement of regional integration in East Asia. Our final consideration should be given to the United States as the most important and powerful extra-regional player. Realistically speaking, any kind of East Asian co-operative framework would fail if opposed by the United States since it has been heavily involved in security and economic affairs in the region. In this regard the opening of an EAS and the U.S. policy position towards East Asian co-operation become serious challenges to both ASEAN and Korea.

East Asia Summit

It is not easy to forecast how the process of an EAS will play out. As there are still a number of uncertainties, such as the nature of the relationship between ASEAN plus Three and the EAS, issues of agenda, how often the EAS will be held, and how it will be run. Up to now, with regard to the EAS modalities, it seems that the ASEAN countries internally agree on several points, such as ASEAN's chairmanship of the EAS, once every three years in terms of frequency, and an agenda of political and security issues. But, this in effect hints that the ASEAN countries would not accept the new members as core participants in the existing ASEAN plus Three co-operation process. However, India, in particular, wants to avoid at all cost becoming a second-class member of Asia and is seeking to be incorporated into the inner core of East Asia at whatever price.

It appears that Malaysia and China, as the two main promoters of the EAS, have sought to change the existing ASEAN plus Three summit system into the EAS system as early as possible and deepen the level of regional co-operation among the thirteen member countries. More significantly, it seems that China has pursued some specific plans to set up a strategic consultative forum for the thirteen countries through the EAS, which is to deal with regional security integration matters. Yet, the current situation has the potential to develop in a completely different direction. First of all, it has already been decided that India, Australia, and New Zealand will be included in the EAS, which inevitably leads to a broader concept of East Asian regional co-operation. If India, Australia, and New Zealand participate in the EAS, a new formula of Ten plus Three plus Three regional co-operation will emerge, which could be nothing more than a low-level regional dialogue system. The new formula will be far from the initial concept, as envisioned by China, of a Ten plus Three strategic consultative forum. In other words, there is a strong possibility that the EAS will simply end as a ceremonial procedure.

Certainly, the initiation of the EAS poses a number of questions regarding the future of East Asian co-operation. The most fundamental question is whether the EAS held in Malaysia in 2005 was genuinely an EAS or not. In reports made by the EAVG and EASG, the vision and plan for East Asian regional co-operation was not premised on the expansion of the member countries. However, in its current developmental phase, the EAS does not reflect such a vision but is rather looking more like a post-ASEAN plus Three Summit or a pan-Asia Summit, which is based on expanded membership.

The majority of the ASEAN plus Three countries tend to regard the ASEAN plus Three Summit as a formal and official process for East Asian regional co-operation and see the EAS as an informal and unofficial meeting that could be held once every three years. In addition, many ASEAN plus Three countries prefer to use the EAS as a flexible forum for negotiations and dialogue with countries outside the region, such as India, Australia, and New Zealand. Therefore, many countries in the region have already indicated that the title EAS really has no meaning and are suggesting that the name be changed. Moreover, some experts are arguing that the member states of ASEAN plus Three need to make a concerted effort to realize a truly meaningful EAS in the future.

The U.S. Factor

Although the United States strongly opposed the East Asia Economic Caucus (EAEC) promulgated by former Malaysian Prime Minister Mahathir in the early 1990s and views ASEAN plus Three as a reincarnation of the old EAEC, it has maintained a "wait and see" attitude towards ASEAN plus Three co-operation. There are many reasons for this. The United States foresaw that East Asian co-operation would not work very well due to the lack of regional leadership and significant differences among countries in the region. Thus it had no reason to expect rapid progress or any immediate move towards successful regional integration of ASEAN plus Three co-operation. The United States also hoped that Japan, its strong ally, could take a leading role in developing ASEAN plus Three towards open regionalism.

However, the recent initiative of China to inaugurate the EAS has significantly changed the U.S. position towards East Asian regional integration. The United States began to express its concerns about the possibility of an exclusive and inward-looking EAS and was not quiet about its hope to participate in the summit. Furthermore, the United States tends to regard the EAC as a China-led attempt to demonstrate that Asia no longer wants the United States in the region. By extension, it also perceives that Beijing is attempting to marginalize Washington and ultimately push it out of Asia. Instead of being a member of the EAS, the United States has decided to arrange for more of its allies and strategic partners, such as Australia, New Zealand, and India, to attend the upcoming summit in order to counterbalance China. It seems quite clear that the United States will try to subvert East Asian co-operation or directly involve itself in the process if the ASEAN plus Three and EAS processes are dominated by China or if East Asian states push ahead with discussions on security matters without the participation of Washington.

But the fundamental question is: What does an EAC mean to the United States? East Asia is hopeful that, unlike fifteen years ago, the United States will support regional institutional-building efforts. The United States needs to understand that an EAC is coming to a head much faster than expected, and it is basically a sort of natural phenomenon, albeit sometimes forged by governmental actions. Accordingly, the United States should encourage proposals for East Asian co-operation where shared goals of reducing tensions are involved. Doing so would promote free trade and adhere to the rule of law. Whether the United States becomes an integral part of it or not is immaterial because East Asian co-operation will serve the interests of both Asia and the United States. Regional co-operative mechanisms, such as ASEAN plus Three or the EAS, could be an effective way of reducing tensions and preventing potential conflicts among the countries in the region. In addition, East Asian co-operation can ultimately contribute to not only achieving closer economic ties among the nations but also increasing the well-being and welfare of people in the region through various means of co-operation. It also greatly contributes to advancing human security by facilitating regional efforts for environmental protection and good governance. All this will be in the interest of the United States as well.

The continued friction and rivalries among East Asian countries, such as China and Japan, may not necessarily hurt U.S. interests. They may present an obstacle to the EAC, at least in the short term, or they may bring Japan closer to the United States. On the whole, however, they will not serve the interests of the United States either because East Asia, particularly Northeast Asia, will become unstable. To be sure, the United States will nevertheless be blamed for fostering discord among the East Asian countries.

REFERENCES

Ba, Alica. "The Politics and Economics of 'East Asia' in ASEAN-China Relations". In *China and Southeast Asia. Global Changes and Regional Challenges*, edited by Ho Khai Leong and Samuel Ku. Singapore: Institute of Southeast Asian Studies, 2005.

Goh, Evelyn. *Meeting the China Challenge, The US in Southeast Asian Regional Security Strategies*. Washington, D.C.: East-West Center, 2005.

Han, Sung-Joo. "Roadmap for an East Asian Community". IRI Review 10, no. 2 (2005).

Hew, Denis and Rahul Sen. *Towards an ASEAN Economic Community: Challenges and Prospects*. Singapore: Institute of Southeast Asian Studies, 2004.

Severino, Rodolfo C. *Towards an ASEAN Security Community*. Singapore: Institute of Southeast Asian Studies, 2004.

Siddique, Sharon and Sree Kumar, compilers. *The 2nd ASEAN Reader*. Singapore: Institute of Southeast Asian Studies, 2003.

INDEX

.